The Creative Marketer

The Chartered Institite of Marketing/Butterworth-Heinemann Marketing Series is the most comprehensive, widely used and important collection of books in marketing and sales currently available worldwide.

As the CIM's official publisher, Butterworth-Heinemann develops, produces and publishes the complete series in association with the CIM. We aim to provide definitive marketing books for students and practitioners that promote excellence in marketing education and practice.

The series titles are written by CIM senior examiners and leading marketing educators for professionals, students and those studying the CIM's Certificate, Advanced Certificate and Postgraduate Diploma courses. Now firmly established, these titles provide practical study support to CIM and other marketing students and to practitioners at all levels.

 The Chartered
Institute of Marketing

Formed in 1911, The Chartered Institute of Marketing is now the largest professional marketing management body in the world with over 60,000 members located worldwide. Its primary objectives are focused on the development of awareness and understanding of marketing throughout UK industry and commerce and in the raising of standards of professionalism in the education, training and practice of this key business discipline.

Books in the series

The Creative Marketer

Simon Majaro

Published in association with The
Chartered Institute of Marketing

Butterworth-Heinemann
Linacre House, Jordan Hill, Oxford OX2 8DP
225 Wildwood Avenue, Woburn, MA 01801-2041
A division of Reed Educational and Professional Publishing Ltd

℞ A member of the Reed Elsevier plc group

OXFORD   BOSTON   JOHANNESBURG
MELBOURNE   NEW DELHI   SINGAPORE

First published 1991
Paperback edition 1993
Reprinted 1996, 1997, 1998

© Simon Majaro 1991

British Library Cataloguing in Publication Data
A catalogue record for this book is available from the British Library

ISBN 0 7506 1708 X

Printed and bound in Great Britain by
MPG Books Ltd, Bodmin, Cornwall

CONTENTS

PREFACE

Few topics in management thought and practice evoke more interest, and even excitement, than the subject of creativity. The moment one utters the word 'Creativity' to any audience the image of a group of long-haired, flashily-dressed, idea-generating individuals springs to mind.

One often assumes that creativity is the prerogative of the select few upon whom a special gift has been bestowed by the Almighty. One tends to associate this gift with people working in product design, advertising agencies or other activities that call for a 'creative content' to their output. Similarly one takes for granted that architects must be 'creative'; yet one is not prepared to suppose that accountants, lawyers and actuaries are capable of a similar gift.

In the business world the notion that creativity can only be found in a small number of corners or pockets of the organisation is not an uncommon belief. Indeed it is often postulated that those associated with the marketing function are more likely to be creative than members of other functions like production, finance and others. This book seeks to explode this myth.

Creativity is not a minority talent. Creativity can be learnt and improved in the same way as one can improve one's ability to learn foreign languages. In the right environment and with the appropriate stimulation and motivation most people can become more creative. Nevertheless it is important to recognise that the essential element in achieving a greater creative output is the existence of a steadfast desire to attain such an aim. In the context of a company this aim must be promulgated by the firm's leaders. It is difficult for an individual to practise his or her creativity within a firm that considers creative people as members of a troublesome species.

Is there a benefit for a company in becoming more creative? I am yet to meet a manager who would say 'No' in response to this question. It is universally assumed that enhanced creativity can provide a company with a competitive edge. The astounding fact is that a small number of companies actually take steps to develop the organisation's creative processes. The desire to do something about it is commonplace; the practical application of the developmental activities called for is a minority practice.

Over the years I have worked with many companies who invited me to attempt to improve the creativity of their organisations and their personnel. I discovered that before one can improve the firm's performance in this regard one must attempt to audit the level of creativity that

PREFACE

exists in the organisation at a given point of time. With this objective in mind I developed a detailed list of audit questionnaires designed to assess the creativity and innovation levels of the firm at corporate level and also in all other functional areas. To the extent that I consider marketing people as the champions of creativity in any organisation I felt that it was appropriate to provide them with a system which would enable them to evaluate the level of creativity in other departments. After all, it is inconceivable for marketers to enjoy the fruits of their creativity without the whole-hearted participation in the whole process of other functions, such as R & D, production, finance and so on.

This book covers in detail the whole process of managing ideas from gestation to implementation – from creativity to innovation. The aim is to provide the marketer with material which is capable of immediate and practical applicability. Step-by-step procedures are explained in simple terms and some worksheets are provided for individual and group use.

The book consists of seven parts. Each part can be used as a stand-alone workbook with supportive exercises, tables and work-sheets. The content follows a logical sequence of knowledge-acquisition and work-procedure:

I believe that those who decide to follow all the parts in the sequence in which they are presented and complete all the exercises and work-procedures with diligence will derive considerable benefit from the process. The benefit will manifest itself in the ability to manage the creativity and innovation processes of the firm in general, and the marketing department in particular, in a more effective way.

The important point to remember is that this book is not meant to be read as a textbook. It should be treated as a permanent companion to the management of the firm's creativity and innovation. Those who use it in this spirit should find it a most valuable aid to personal effectiveness.

In assembling this book I received a lot of help and encouragement from colleagues and students at the Cranfield School of Management. I should like to express to them all a collective 'thank you' through these pages. In particular I should like to thank John Leppard who demonstrated considerable creativity in placing all the concepts and techniques into a 'user-friendly' format.

INTRODUCTION

This book is about creativity and innovation. Highly successful companies are innovators because in order to make the quantum leap which sets them apart from their competitors they have to be venturesome and bold. Superior performance comes from staying ahead of the competition. Small improvements to products and operations tend to yield only small improvements to profits, whereas big ones generate big profits.

If the rate of change outside an organisation exceeds the rate of change inside, then that organisation will go the way of the dodo. To stay in business a company has to respond creatively to the problems it faces. Here are just a few external conditions which create problems for businesses:

- slow growth in the economy
- high interest rates
- high exchange rates
- increased levels of foreign competition
- crowded high-growth markets
- too many 'me-too' products
- new technological developments
- new legislation and/or deregulation
- shorter product life cycles
- skill shortages in key areas.

In addition to unfavourable or volatile external conditions, businesses face internal problems such as:

- poor communications
- poorly demarcated or ill-understood chains of responsibility
- financial problems
- imbalances or shortages in staff skills
- technical challenges
- unproductive internal politics
- poor corporate image
- alienated or poorly motivated staff
- low sales
- insufficient forward planning.

In order to combat these and other problems facing the organisation, its creative brainpower will have to be recognised and developed.
Which is why this book has been produced.

Problem-solving, creativity and innovation

To many people the words 'creativity' and 'innovation' are virtually synonymous and interchangeable. This is not the way these words are used here, so it is appropriate to define our terms at the outset. Creativity is an aid to problem-solving. It can bring new insights about the nature of a problem and provide a wide range of options from which the most appropriate solution may be chosen. Innovation, by contrast, represents the creative solution itself, a change introduced to remedy a problem or improve a situation. In brief then:

Creativity is the thinking process which helps us generate ideas.

Innovation is the practical application of such ideas towards performing a task in a better way.

Creativity is thus the raw material or input to innovation, whereas innovation is the commercial or technological outcome. Creativity can be eccentric and know no bounds, but innovation must always be practical and capable of yielding tangible results. Novelty per se is not necessarily innovative in character. To pursue an idea just because it is creative and original will be non-productive if ultimately it is going to cost more or do the job in a less satisfactory way. For these reasons, this guide to creativity and innovation describes techniques both for generating and for screening ideas, to help you find optimal solutions to your business problems.

Creativity can be divided into three categories, depending on how it originates. These three types of creativity are: **normative creativity, exploratory creativity and creativity by serendipity.**

Normative creativity

Creativity is said to be normative when ideas are sought to solve specific needs, problems or objectives. Because normative creativity is focused in this way, it is often considered to be more cost-effective than other forms of creativity. It is particularly suited to predictive aspects of marketing which are concerned to find better products and services to meet future needs.

The mere fact that creative effort is focused can produce a 'blinkered' effect, narrowing the field of creative vision. Thus normative creativity by its very nature may be a constraint on the full range of human imagination and idea-generation.

A number of tools and techniques to help the creative problem-solver are provided in Section 5.

Exploratory creativity

Creativity is said to be exploratory when ideas are generated which are not necessarily related to known requirements or demands. Exploratory creativity reveals opportunities which are not always exploitable in commercial terms, whereas normative creativity is result-orientated. Nevertheless, such freewheeling creative-thinking techniques can often uncover 'buried treasure' in terms of valuable ideas.

Exploratory creativity is particularly useful for extrapolating from current knowledge and technology towards the future. Whether the outcome of such 'visioning' is perceived as a threat or an opportunity is not the issue. What is important is that this type of activity can help an organisation extract itself from a strategic rut or get into better shape for an admittedly uncertain, but undoubtedly different, future.

A synthesis of normative and exploratory creativity provides the ideal combination of goal-orientation and imaginative richness.

A number of exploratory creative techniques such as morphological analysis, scenario writing and scenario day-dreaming are described in Section 5.

Creativity by serendipity

Creativity and the innovation that may result from it are said to take place by serendipity when the idea underlying the innovation is discovered by happy accident. The word 'serendipity' was taken from a novel by Horace Walpole, *The Three Princes of Serendip* (an ancient name of Sri Lanka), in which the heroes were 'always making discoveries of things they were not in quest of.'

The world of fiction aside, many important scientific breakthroughs have originated in this way. Most of us remember the stories we learned at school about the apple dropping on Isaac Newton's head, Archimedes leaping out of his bath shouting 'Eureka!' at the notion of water displacement, or the young James Watt observing the kettle lid being forced upwards by rising steam as the kettle boiled on the hob. Even though the popular myths surrounding such discoveries may fail to do justice to the preparatory thought and training leading up to them, they do convey an important element of truth: that a perceptive mind endowed with curiosity and imagination can sometimes experience flashes of creative insight.

Creativity by serendipity is not the sole domain of geniuses. Every one of us may experience these sudden insights at times. Many brilliant, but not necessarily earth-shattering, innovations emerge every day as a result of ordinary individuals responding to chance events in a creative way.

Since by definition this form of creativity is random and dependent on outside influences, it is not possible to provide tools or techniques to induce it. Yet the creativity techniques discussed in section 5 can encourage a receptive attitude which would allow such chance insights to be recognised and developed if they should occur.

The Problem-solving process

The following figure describes a typical problem-solving routine and indicates some of the techniques described in this manual that can be useful in this process.

Sometimes the solution to one problem gives rise to another. For example, in a case where the initial problem was to find a more effective advertising campaign for a product range, the subsequent success of the new advertising might increase demand so much that labour supply, funding, storage and distribution all become new problems. Thus the sequence described in Figure 1 can be considered either as a single process or as one which is repeated over a number of cycles.

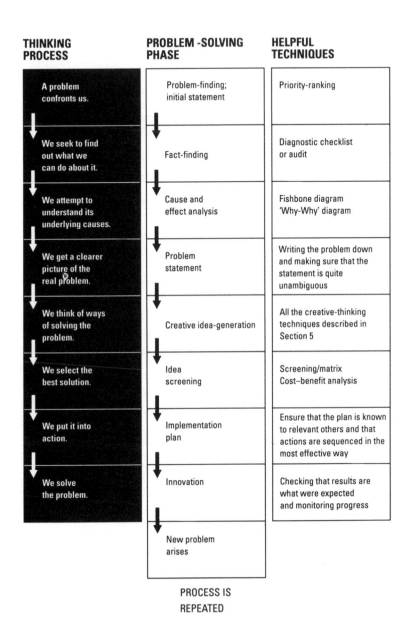

THINKING PROCESS	PROBLEM -SOLVING PHASE	HELPFUL TECHNIQUES
A problem confronts us.	Problem-finding; initial statement	Priority-ranking
We seek to find out what we can do about it.	Fact-finding	Diagnostic checklist or audit
We attempt to understand its underlying causes.	Cause and effect analysis	Fishbone diagram 'Why-Why' diagram
We get a clearer picture of the real problem.	Problem statement	Writing the problem down and making sure that the statement is quite unambiguous
We think of ways of solving the problem.	Creative idea-generation	All the creative-thinking techniques described in Section 5
We select the best solution.	Idea screening	Screening/matrix Cost–benefit analysis
We put it into action.	Implementation plan	Ensure that the plan is known to relevant others and that actions are sequenced in the most effective way
We solve the problem.	Innovation	Checking that results are what were expected and monitoring progress
	New problem arises	

PROCESS IS
REPEATED

Figure 1   The problem-solving process

2 AUDITS

In this section you are asked to answer a number of questions regarding aspects of creativity in your organisation. The questions are phrased in such a way that either 'Yes' or 'No' is the obvious answer. However, since the situation in any organisation is rarely so black or white, there are a range of possible answers along the spectrum between 'Yes' and 'No', indicating various shades of grey, as shown below.

Creativity Audit at Corporate Level

Select your score for each question and enter it in the box provided.

Your Answer	No	Rarely	Sometimes	Often	Yes
Points	0	1	2	3	4

1 Does the organisation's Mission Statement mention 'creativity', 'innovation' or both as being part of the corporate ethos?

2 Is top management involved and actively interested in the process of generating ideas?

3 Is the organisational climate supportive of the idea-generation process?

4 Can staff approach top management with ideas and get a fair hearing?

5 Do people in the organisation talk about 'creativity', 'ideas' and 'innovation'?

6 Do people in the organisation know where to take their ideas?

7 Does the organisation undertake regular training or idea-generating exercises in order to stimulate the overall climate for creativity?

8 Does the organisation undertake regular training or idea-generating exercises in order to solve problems and/or identify opportunities?

9 Does a communication system exist for 'marketing' the corporate approach to creativity and innovation?

10 Does the organisation actively encourage communication and cross-fertilisation of ideas:

■ between different levels of the organisation?

■ between different functions?

■* between different operating units?

■* between different international markets?

(* score only if appropriate)

11 Is there a system (as opposed to ad-hoc arrangements) for screening and evaluating ideas in the organisation?

12 Is the number of innovations at corporate level considered to be satisfactory?

13 In general, is the level of creativity and innovation in the following functional areas satisfactory:

■ Marketing ?

■ Production ?

■ Personnel ?

■ Research and Development ?

■ Finance ?

■ Central Administration/Services ?

TOTAL

Scoring the Creativity Audit at Corporate Level

1 Add up the total points scored and enter this figure in the box.

2 The highest possible number of points is 76 (if the last two items under Question 10 were not applicable) or 84 (if all questions were scored).

3 Calculate the total points scored as a percentage of the maximum, and enter this percentage in the box. This is your score.

$$\boxed{\quad\quad\%}$$

4 Your score can be interpreted as follows:

Less than 25%

The level of creativity is very low. Unless the organisation operates in extremely stable markets, its long-term survival must be held in question. Some action should be taken to improve the situation – **NOW**.

25%–50%

This represents a fair level of creativity, typical of many organisations, but it will be essential to make improvements if the business is to remain competitive.

51%–75%

This score is good to very good, but should not be taken as an invitation to complacency. Improvement is still possible and further efforts to extend creativity are likely to be well worthwhile.

Over 75%

Excellent to superb. The main challenge facing the organisation will be to maintain creativity at this high level.

Comparative Creativity Audit at Functional Level

The scoring system operates in the same way as for the previous Audit.

Your Answer	No	Rarely	Sometimes	Often	Yes
Points	0	1	2	3	4

Functional Areas

	Marketing	Production	Personnel	Research & Development	Finance	Central Administration
1 Is the general climate within the department or function supportive of the process of generating ideas?						
2 Does the top management of the department take an active interest in idea-generation, as opposed to just sitting back and waiting for others to come up with ideas?						
3 Do the department's objectives mention 'creativity' or 'innovation', or both?						
4 Do people in the department talk about 'creativity', 'ideas' and 'innovation'?						
5 Is the top management of the department approachable and receptive to ideas?						
6 Do people in the department know how and to whom they can submit their ideas?						

	Functional Areas						
	Marketing	Production	Personnel	Research & Development	Finance	Central Administration	

7 Does the department undertake regular training or use 'idea-generating' exercises in order to stimulate creativity?

8 Does the department undertake regular training or use 'idea-generating' exercises in order to solve problems and/or identify opportunities?

9 Does a system exist for 'marketing' the concepts of 'creativity' and 'innovation' throughout the department?

10 Does the department attempt to communicate and cross-fertilise ideas with other departments, units, etc.?

11 Does a system exist for screening and evaluating ideas in the department?

12 Is the number of innovations produced by the department considered to be satisfactory?

TOTAL

Scoring the Comparative Audit

This Audit shows at a glance the comparative creativity of each department. You may wish simply to compare the 'raw' scores or to use the more elaborate percentage system and method of interpretation shown in the previous Audit. (The maximum number of points for each functional area is 48.) In either case, the Audit indicates the areas within the organisation which could benefit most from an improvement in creativity.

The specific aspects of creativity within each organisational function can be assessed in the following Area Audits.

Marketing Audit

Select your score for each question and enter it in the box provided.

Your Answer	No	Rarely	Sometimes	Often	Yes
Points	0	1	2	3	4

Information-gathering activities

1 Has the marketing department recently developed better or cheaper ways of collecting information than in the past?

2 Does the marketing management monitor the costs and benefits of data collection and input, and seek to improve their pay-off value?

3 Are the relative costs of in-house marketing research and fees to an outside agency for comparable work known and acted upon?

Product policy and planning

4 Is the organisation's record of new product/service development satisfactory when compared with its main competitors?

5 Is the success rate of new products or services satisfactory?

6 Is the speed at which ideas are converted into practical innovations improving?

Pricing

7 Is pricing used creatively to give the organisation a distinctive position in the market, as opposed to being merely the application of a formula?

8 Does the marketing department observe the practices of other companies in order to help solve difficult pricing problems?

9 Has the marketing team overcome pricing problems by using creative 'non-price' strategies?

Promotional mix

10 Has the level of creativity demonstrated in the promotional mix over the last few years been high?

11 Has the cost–benefit ratio of promotional campaigns improved in recent years?

12 Does the organisation develop its own promotional ideas, as opposed to relying on outside agencies to do the creative thinking?

13 Does the organisation experiment with new communication ideas (such as new technology) on a fairly regular basis?

14 Does the marketing management effectively scan and identify good ideas used in its own or other markets?

Distribution

15 Has the organisation been able to improve the quality and/or reduce the cost of logistics in recent years?

16 Has the organisation evaluated alternative channels of distribution in order to improve customer satisfaction?

17 Has the organisation been able to improve the loyalty of its intermediaries and improve service to customers in recent years?

18 Does the marketing team involve the channel intermediaries in the process of idea-generation and/or strategy planning?

19 Is the organisation's distribution sufficiently creative compared with that of its main competitors?

Sales

20 Is the sales force sufficiently creative?

21 Is there a procedure for cross-fertilising ideas between sales regions, offices and the like?

22 Are members of the sales force involved in idea-generating activities in response to problems in other departments?

23 Does sales management attempt to identify what 'star salespeople' do which is different from the rest of the sales force?

24 Are salespeople sufficiently motivated to submit ideas for evaluation?

25 Has sales management been able to improve the ratio of customer-contact time to travel in recent years?

Marketing control procedures

26 Has the organisation been creative in the way that it controls its various marketing activities (for example, sales effectiveness, advertising or promotional effectiveness and so on)?

27 Does the organisation react quickly to competitive threats?

28 Can the organisation respond quickly to market opportunities?

TOTAL

Scoring the Marketing Audit

1 Add the total to the 'raw' score for Marketing from the Comparative Creativity Audit at Functional Level.

Marketing Audit Total   Comparative Audit Total   Grand Total

$$\boxed{} \quad + \quad \boxed{} \quad = \quad \boxed{}$$

2 Calculate the Grand Total as a percentage of the maximum points available, 160 (i.e. 112 + 48). Enter this figure in the box. This is your score.

$$\boxed{\qquad \% \;}$$

3 The interpretation of your score is similar to that for the Creativity Audit at Corporate Level.

Less than **25%**

Poor. Urgent action required.

25%–50%

Fair, but improvement is essential.

51%–75%

Good to very good, but improvement is still possible with hard work.

Over **75%**

Excellent to superb, but keep at it.

Production Audit

Select your score for each question and enter it in the box provided.

Your Answer	No	Rarely	Sometimes	Often	Yes
Points	0	1	2	3	4

Quality

1 Can the production department demonstrate examples of creative improvements in quality?

2 Are 'Quality Circles' used as a way of solving quality problems?

3 Are production personnel encouraged to discover and analyse the quality-control procedures of competitors?

4 Have investigations been carried out to check whether customers are happy with the quality improvements introduced (i.e. are improvements customer-orientated)?

Materials handling and logistics

5 Has performance improved in the area of materials handling?

6 Have new ideas about stock control and the availability of materials and components (such as the 'Just in Time' method) been put into practice?

7 Has material usage become more efficient and/or has scrap been reduced?

8 Does the production department respond effectively to customers' delivery needs?

9 Has the quality of physical distribution been improved?

10 Are fewer complaints received about goods damaged in transit?

Productivity

11 Are ideas for improvements in productivity explored at all levels of the department?

12 Have steps been taken to conserve energy in an innovative way?

13 Are comparative studies undertaken to identify ideas for productivity improvements used by competitors?

New technology

14 Does the production department have a record of recommending and adopting methods associated with new technology?

15 Does the department understand and learn from the practices of its competitors, with respect to new technology?

16 Is the organisation getting satisfactory benefits from the application of new technology?

Plant and facilities

17 Is there a record of continual improvement in the area of plant maintenance and preventive maintenance?

18 Has the department demonstrated creativity in the choice of plant layout and/or the location of new production units?

CREATIVITY & INNOVATION 2. AUDITS

19 Does the department have a good safety record and try to be proactive in the fields of accident-prevention and safety education?

20 Does the department have a good record with regard to environmental issues such as noise, pollution and so on?

TOTAL

Scoring the Production Audit

1 Add the total to the 'raw' score for Production from the Comparative Creativity Audit at Functional Level.

Productivity Audit Total   Comparative Audit Total   Grand Total

$$\boxed{} \quad + \quad \boxed{} \quad = \quad \boxed{}$$

2 Calculate the Grand Total as a percentage of the maximum points available, 128 (i.e. 80 + 48). Enter this figure in the box. This is your score.

$$\boxed{ \%}$$

3 The interpretation of your score is similar to that for the Creativity Audit at Corporate Level.

Less than **25%**

Poor. Urgent action required.

25%–50%

Fair, but improvement is essential.

51%–75%

Good to very good, but improvement is still possible with hard work.

Over **75%**

Excellent to superb, but keep at it.

Personnel Audit

Select your score for each question and enter it in the box provided.

Your Answer	No	Rarely	Sometimes	Often	Yes
Points	0	1	2	3	4

Motivation

1 Has the personnel department experimented with new and better ways to motivate all company employees?

2 In general, are existing incentive packages innovative?

3 Are creative steps taken to improve or maintain morale throughout the organisation?

4 Is the department seen as a source of good ideas when other departments have problems with staff motivation?

5 Has the department recommended creative non-financial components in the total employee 'remuneration package'?

6 Has the department initiated creative programmes in the sphere of advisory work and personnel welfare (such as drug or alcohol counselling, stress management services and the like)?

Personnel productivity

7 Has the department taken steps to improve its own level of productivity?

8 Has the department made a creative contribution to improvements in the productivity of other departments?

9 Has the department been proactive in identifying factors such as skill shortages, which would reduce organisational efficiency?

Staff recruitment

10 Has the department been innovative in the field of recruitment and selection procedures?

11 Is the cost of recruitment known and are steps being taken to reduce it, or improve its effectiveness?

12 Have creative ideas been used in communicating company information to prospective recruits and/or new employees?

Management development

13 Does the department demonstrate creativity in assessing the number and needs of managers in the future?

14 Have the organisation's management-development and training systems benefited from innovative thinking?

15 Has the department taken steps to motivate managers to pursue programmes of self-development?

16 Has the department been creative in selecting and working with outside training agencies?

17 Has the department been successful in facilitating the return to work of managers who have been on courses, so that they can put their new learning into practice?

18 Is the training and development of managers being achieved in a better, more cost-effective way than previously?

Industrial relations

19 Has the department demonstrated a more creative approach to industrial relations than in the past?

20 Has the relationship between management and labour improved as a result of the department's approach to industrial relations?

21 Has the record of days lost, whether due to strikes or general absenteeism, improved as a result of the personnel department's input?

Working conditions

22 Are improvements in the organisation's work environment regularly initiated?

23 Are suggestions about improving working conditions actively sought by the department (for example, through suggestion schemes and the like)?

24 Have improved working conditions led to higher output and/or fewer accidents?

25 Have any recent innovations provided better leisure or recreational facilities for the organisation's personnel?

TOTAL

Scoring the Personnel Audit

1 Add the total to the 'raw' score for Personnel from the Comparative Creativity Audit at Functional Level.

Personnel Audit Total   Comparative Audit Total   Grand Total

[ ]   **+**   [ ]   **=**   [ ]

2 Calculate the Grand Total as a percentage of the maximum points available, 148 (i.e. 100 + 48). Enter this figure in the box. This is your score.

[%   ]

3 The interpretation of your score is similar to that for the Creativity Audit at Corporate Level.

Less than **25%**

Poor. Urgent action required.

25%–50%

Fair, but improvement is essential.

51%–75%

Good to very good, but improvement is still possible with hard work.

Over **75%**

Excellent to superb, but keep at it.

Research and Development Audit

Select your score for each question and enter it in the box provided.

Your Answer	No	Rarely	Sometimes	Often	Yes
Points	0	1	2	3	4

Productivity

1 Has the R & D department been more productive through the use of newer and/or better methods?

2 Does the department respond more quickly than in the past to demands placed on it by other departments?

3 Is the 'rate of exchange' between results and expenditure on R & D known and is it improving?

4 Has the R & D department filed an increasing number of patents in the last two years compared with earlier years?

Product innovations

5 Has the department contributed to the development of cheaper and/or better products?

6 Has the department been a key contributor to solving quality problems?

7 Has R & D helped to identify and sustain a competitive advantage in the firm's product strategy?

8 Does the department continually monitor potential innovations by scanning competitors' activities, the educational and scientific world, and the market-place at large?

Interaction with other functions

9 Does the department interact with other departments, especially marketing and production, in a creative way?

10 Is this creative collaboration improving overall?

11 Does R & D 'market' its own image in a creative way?

12 Do other departments automatically approach R & D when they have technical problems with products and/or their processing?

Recruiting talent

13 Does the department have a record of attracting the right kind of recruits?

14 Does the department use creative measures to improve its attractiveness to potential recruits?

15 Does the department compare favourably with key competitors in its ability to attract and retain staff?

16 Do people progress in the department on the basis of the creativity they bring to their work?

TOTAL

Scoring the Research and Development Audit

1 Add the total to the 'raw' score for R & D from the Comparative Creativity Audit at Functional Level.

R & D Audit Total   Comparative Audit Total   Grand Total

□ **+** □ **=** □

2 Calculate the Grand Total as a percentage of the maximum points available, 112 (i.e. 64 + 48). Enter this figure in the box. This is your score.

□ %

3 The interpretation of your score is similar to that for the Creativity Audit at Corporate Level.

Less than **25%**

Poor. Urgent action required.

25%–50%

Fair, but improvement is essential.

51%–75%

Good to very good, but improvement is still possible with hard work.

Over **75%**

Excellent to superb, but keep at it.

Finance Audit

Select your score for each question and enter it in the box provided.

Your Answer	No	Rarely	Sometimes	Often	Yes
Points	0	1	2	3	4

Accounting and control

1 Has the department put into practice more effective and cost-beneficial methods of data collection and storage?

2 Does the department respond positively to suggestions from outside sources (auditors, consultants, VAT inspectors and so on) as to how accounting and control systems can be improved?

3 Are the financial and accounting systems of the firm regularly reviewed to see how they might be improved?

Reporting

4 Does the department exploit opportunities provided by changes in accounting and regulatory pronouncements to improve the reporting of financial information?

5 Does the finance department seek to influence decisions on accounting standards and reporting within the industry?

6 Does the department have a record of experimenting with better ways to present information?

7 Does the department make a creative contribution towards making better use of the organisation's annual report as an aid to promoting the corporate image?

Treasury

8 Are people in the finance function aware of modern developments in financing such as swaps and the like? □

9 Does the department use innovative funding methods to reduce costs or risk for the organisation? □

Taxation

10 Does the department use creativity in developing schemes to minimise the company's tax charges? □

Project appraisal

11 Are members of the finance function involved, on their own initiative, as members of multi-disciplinary project-appraisal teams? □

12 In general are members of the department viewed by other departments as creative contributors to the success of the business (as opposed to being 'score-keepers')? □

13 Is the department a source of creative ideas for improving organisational performance? □

Productivity

14 Does the department make creative contributions to methods of inventory control, cost control and so on? □

15 Does the department take steps to improve the productivity of its own personnel through simpler systems, reduced paperwork, better use of existing data and the like? □

Recruitment

16 Does the department attract talented recruits and retain their services? □

TOTAL □

Scoring the Finance Audit

1 Add the total to the 'raw' score for Finance from the Comparative Creativity Audit at Functional Level.

Finance Audit Total   Comparative Audit Total   Grand Total

$$\boxed{} \quad + \quad \boxed{} \quad = \quad \boxed{}$$

2 Calculate the Grand Total as a percentage of the maximum points available, 112 (i.e. 64 + 48). Enter this figure in the box. This is your score.

$$\boxed{\qquad\qquad \%}$$

3 The interpretation of your score is similar to that for the Creativity Audit at Corporate Level.

Less than **25%**

Poor. Urgent action required.

25%–50%

Fair, but improvement is essential.

51%–75%

Good to very good, but improvement is still possible with hard work.

Over **75%**

Excellent to superb, but keep at it.

Central Admistration and Services Audit

Select your score for each question and enter it in the box provided.

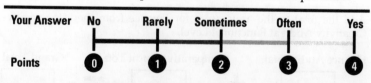

Your Answer	No	Rarely	Sometimes	Often	Yes
Points	0	1	2	3	4

Since this area can vary greatly from one company to another, this Audit is designed to provide an indication of how creativity might be evaluated, rather than a rigid assessment. By developing questions like the ones below, it ought to be possible for an organisation to devise its own Creativity Audit of this function.

1 *Telephone/Telex/Fax*
Have these services benefited from creative improvements in the last few years?

2 *Reception area*
Has the quality of welcome to visitors been improved as the result of some recent innovation?

3 Is there any evidence of creativity or innovation in the general appearance of the reception area?

4 Is there any evidence of creativity or innovation in the landscaping or general external appearance of the premises (especially the areas that make an impact on visitors)?

5 *Gatehouse and security*
Have there been recent improvements in the way the gatehouse staff manage the entry and exit of visitors and staff?

6 Has security become more effective and less intrusive as the result of adopting new ideas and/or approaches?

General

7 Have there been any recent innovations in office cleaning?

8 Have there been any recent innovations in the cleaning and maintenance of washrooms and toilets?

9 Have the issues of the adequacy and quality of car-parking facilities been addressed in creative ways?

10 Have the quality, service and general performance of the canteen improved recently as the result of new ideas being implemented?

11 Are there indications of better energy conservation as a result of using creative strategies?

Secretarial/Administrative services

12 Are secretaries/administrators encouraged to be involved in the organisation's creative processes?

13 Is there evidence of improvements in services provided by secretaries and administrators as a result of this involvement?

14 Is the working partnership between managers and secretaries based on the free flow of ideas?

15 Are creative ideas being used to reduce paperwork and photocopying costs?

16 Is new technology used to make office work more interesting, instead of repetitive and mundane?

TOTAL

Scoring the Central Administration Audit

1 Add the total to the 'raw' score for Central Administration from the Comparative Creativity Audit at Functional Level.

Central Administration Audit   Comparative Audit Total   Grand Total

[ ]   **+**   [ ]   **=**   [ ]

2 Calculate the Grand Total as a percentage of the maximum points available. If all of the questions were answered, this is 112 (i.e. 64 + 48). If only some of the questions were relevant to your organisation, calculate the appropriate maximum and work out your score from this figure. Enter your score in the box.

[%]

3 The interpretation of your score is similar to that for the Creativity Audit at Corporate Level.

Less than **25%**

Poor. Urgent action required.

25%–50%

Fair, but improvement is essential.

51%–75%

Good to very good, but improvement is still possible with hard work.

Over **75%**

Excellent to superb, but keep at it.

In this section you have analysed the level of creativity in your organisation by completing a number of Creativity Audits. Two of these Audits focused on your organisation as a whole:

- the Creativity Audit at Corporate Level and
- the Comparative Creativity Audit at Functional Level.

There were also six Area Audits focusing on the various specific functions of your organisation:

- Marketing
- Production
- Personnel
- Research and Development
- Finance
- Central Administration and Services.

You may find it helpful to make a summary of your findings in the spaces provided.

STRENGTHS   In terms of creativity, our greatest strengths
appear to be:

WEAKNESSES In terms of creativity, our greatest weaknesses appear to be:

OPPORTUNITIES Our strengths make it possible for us to:

THREATS Our weaknesses are likely to make us vulnerable to:

Creativity Audits Action Plan

Action	PRIORITY			Starting date	By me	By others (name)	Comments about progress/ outcome
	High	Medium	Low				
1							
2							
3							
4							
5							
6							
7							
8							
9							
10							
11							
12							
13							
14							
15							

3 CLIMATE

Creative people blossom in creative environments. Individual creativity is never really extinguished, even in hostile environments, but in such situations creative people usually stay quiet and keep their good ideas to themselves. Or they become alienated and use their creativity against the unreceptive organisation. If the situation becomes too frustrating, they eventually leave and join an organisation where they can exercise their creative talents openly and legitimately.

What are the signals which tell creative individuals that their organisation does not really value creativity (regardless of what top management might claim)? One study of how leaders of organisations develop and transmit corporate cultures or climates identified several 'reinforcing mechanisims' (Schein, 1985). Whether they do so by accident or design, corporate leaders are sending out messages all the time about what they believe is really important, even through such indirect means as architecture and office design, or the jokes they tell (or laugh at) in the boardroom. The full range of these primary and secondary reinforcing mechanisms is shown in Figure 3.

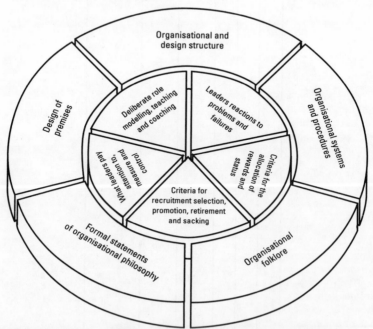

Figure 3 How leaders transmit and entrench corporate culture

Let's analyse each of the primary reinforcment mechanisms for what it can tell us about leadership's attitude to creativity.

How often does the top management pay attention to or show genuine concern about creativity and creative ideas?

In creative organisations the leaders react positively to new ideas, are always looking for ways to stimulate creativity, and, above all, show their commitment by setting up new initiatives and monitoring their progress with interest, not merely in order to maintain control.

How often is creativity rewarded either in financial terms or by some enhancement of status?

If creativity is not rewarded, and other things are, then it is reasonable to assume that these other things are valued more highly in the organisation than it is. In creative organisations creativity often features in employees' annual job appraisals and can, as a result, have salary implications. Creative problem-solving can also feature in special project work or assignments and can thus have an impact on career-development and promotion.

Does creativity feature in the criteria for recruiting new staff or promoting existing personnel? Are people kept at the company, regardless of other shortcomings, because their creative input is valuable and would otherwise be missed?

Creative organisations value creative employees and actively seek to recruit and retain them in-house, rather than merely 'buying-in' creative input from outside when the need for it is recognised.

Do the leaders encourage creativity by providing training for their staff and/or by personally nurturing it in their subordinates?

Actions speak louder than words. Many management skills are learned by subordinates copying a 'role model', who is often their boss. A senior manager who leads from the front when it comes to creativity can have a tremendous impact on the rest of the organisation.

How do the leaders respond when creative ideas or innovations are unsuccessful?

Innovation, by definition, means breaking new ground. To do something new will always entail an element of risk. However, it is only the incompetent manager who, for example, champions a new product or service without assessing and trying to mimimise that risk. Yet things can go wrong, as the failure rate of new products, estimated at 96%, attests.

WHAT HAPPENS THEN

Is the person responsible for the innovation fired to 'discourage' the others? Or is the failure examined in detail so that the organisation as a whole can learn from its mistakes? If a scapegoat has to be sacrificed every time something new fails, people working in the organisation quickly size up the situation and conclude that being innovative in this company can be extremely dangerous. They take up a more defensive posture and top management finds that the flow of ideas from below dries up.

Now let us look at how the secondary reinforcement mechanisms can shape the creative climate in an organisation.

Does the overall structure and design of the organisation promote creativity by minimising bureaucratic procedures and maximising the ease of communicating new ideas?

It is not always fully appreciated that the way a company is structured can have an impact on its overall creative capability. On the whole, small organisations are often more innovative than large ones.

Is the design of the organisation's premises conducive to creativity?

Creative companies recognise that the environment in which people work can have some bearing on their creativity. They attempt to humanise conditions at work, recognising that employees have more respect for themselves and their superiors if they are treated as people rather than as units of production, like machines. After all, it is people not machines who provide ideas.

Wherever possible a stimulating environment should be provided, whether in the architecture of buildings, the design and decoration of work spaces, canteens, and recreational facilities, or the landscaping of company grounds. Grey, blank walls are likely to spawn a grey, blank work-force.

On the other hand, distracting forms of stimulus should be minimised. Few people can think creatively while being deafened in a noisy workshop. A company which takes creativity seriously will provide some quiet areas where people can 'hear themselves think'. If these can't be provided, the company should encourage managers to hold creative meetings away from the workplace.

Does the company include the pursuit and encouragement of creativity and innovation in any of its formal statements of organisational philosophy or corporate aims?

Cynics may say that fine words count for very little. Nevertheless, for the top management of an organisation to make a public, well-publicised statement affirming its stance towards creativity and innovation can do much to bring about a cultural change. It is equally important, of course, that the leaders back these assurances with actions which demonstrate their commitment to creativity.

Do corporate stories, myths and legends indicate that creative individuals, and creativity in general, are highly valued in the organisation?

Often an outsider can gain considerable insight about what is valued in an organisation by asking the deceptively simple question, 'Who are the heroes in this company?', and then asking why. Heroes, myths and legends are all part of an organisation's folklore, which shapes and expresses its own distinctive style. If the stories are about eccentric tyrants who sack people on the spot because they don't like the colour of their tie or some other triviality, it says something about that corporate culture. On the other hand, if the stories are about a person who landed the biggest deal ever, they say something else.

Do the organisation's systems and procedures foster creativity and encourage the communication of ideas so that the best of them can eventually be implemented as innovations?

The creative organisation is always searching for new ideas. Its top management knows that to get one good idea, it will probably have to throw away fifty or more. It knows that hundreds of potential good ideas are locked away in the minds of its workers and their families, its agents and distributors, its customers and the world at large. So it deliberately sets out to establish a self-replenishing pool of ideas from a variety of sources, so that it can pick and choose the best ones. This entails setting up appropriate systems and procedures, such as the following:

- establishing a dynamic suggestion scheme which operates along the lines suggested on page 126
- surveying customers and intermediaries on a regular basis, either face-to-face or by questionnaire, about the products/services they receive
- analysing customer complaints carefully as a potential source of new ideas
- encouraging creativity groups to meet regularly (these are discussed in Section 4)
- encouraging cross-functional, cross-hierarchical meetings

- regularly rewarding good ideas by publicity in the company magazine, on posters and the like, and/or by some form of prize
- conducting regular 'environmental scans' which take into account developments in the business and technological fields at large, both domestically and internationally
- monitoring competitor activity closely
- providing training in creative problem-solving techniques for staff at all levels.

Other diagnostic techniques

There are also other techniques for assessing a firm's creative climate and how it might be improved. The Creativity Audits from Section 2 provide one method for the detailed analysis of an organisation's performance in terms of creativity. Of course, organisations can also devise their own, customised Creativity Audits designed to assess company-specific factors on strategic, management and operational levels.

The following Marketing Creativity Checklist is an example of a simple but comprehensive evaluation technique rating creativity as high, medium or low against a range of factors. You might want to use this model and the following blank worksheet to design more specific Creativity Checklists for the various departments of your own firm.

Marketing Creativity Checklist

	Rating		
	Low	**Med.**	**High**

Strategic

	Low	Med.	High
Mission Statement	☐	☐	☐
Respond to question 'What business are we in?'	☐	☐	☐
Definition of marketing objectives	☐	☐	☐
Corporate image (external)	☐	☐	☐
Corporate image (internal)	☐	☐	☐
The marketing organisation/structure	☐	☐	☐
Overall marketing strategy	☐	☐	☐
Develop our distinctive competence	☐	☐	☐
Develop a sustainable competitive advantage	☐	☐	☐

Management

	Low	Med.	High
Intelligence-gathering	☐	☐	☐
Market research activities	☐	☐	☐
Product development/improvement	☐	☐	☐
Packaging	☐	☐	☐
Pricing	☐	☐	☐
Distribution systems	☐	☐	☐
Promotions	☐	☐	☐
Advertising	☐	☐	☐
Sales	☐	☐	☐

Operational

	Low	Med.	High
Sales force motivation	☐	☐	☐
Territory planning	☐	☐	☐
Customer service	☐	☐	☐
After-sales service	☐	☐	☐
Customer complaints	☐	☐	☐
Sales training	☐	☐	☐

————————— **Creativity Checklist**

Area

	Rating	
Low	**Med.**	**High**

Strategic

———————————————
———————————————
———————————————
———————————————
———————————————
———————————————
———————————————
———————————————

Management

———————————————
———————————————
———————————————
———————————————
———————————————
———————————————
———————————————
———————————————
———————————————

Operational

———————————————
———————————————
———————————————
———————————————
———————————————
———————————————
———————————————
———————————————

Force-field analysis

Another useful method is called 'force-field analysis'. This technique was originally developed by a social scientist as a means of improving problem diagnosis and problem-solving strategies (Lewin, 1947). It assumes that a problem exists because a situation has deviated from an acceptable norm. Therefore, it should be possible to identify both a set of factors which caused this deviation and a set of factors which limits the extent of the deviation.

Imagine that there exists an instrument called a 'creatometer', which can be used to measure organisational creativity, rather like a thermometer is used to measure temperature. In effect, the creatometer registers the equilibrium between the forces operating to raise the level of creativity and the forces operating to lower it. In Figure 4, the actual level of creativity falls short of the ideal benchmark because negative, restraining forces are pushing it down. The level doesn't drop to zero, however, but balances at a position where the restraining forces are countered by the positive, driving forces.

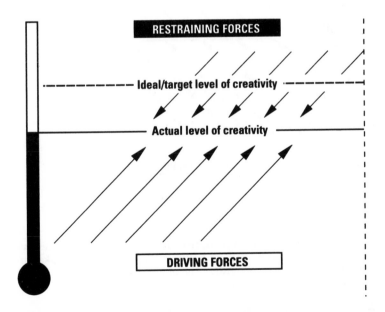

Figure 4   Force-field analysis: the creatometer

Clearly this point of balance could be moved closer to the ideal if some of the restraining forces were reduced and some of the driving forces were enhanced. In practice, if the driving forces are genuine, it is only necessary to remove the restraining forces. It's rather like a ship lying low in the water: it's enough for the crew to jettison some unnecessary cargo to raise the ship's level, without them diving overboard and attempting to lift it up.

If this idea were applied to an organisation, the resulting force-field diagram might look something like Figure 5.

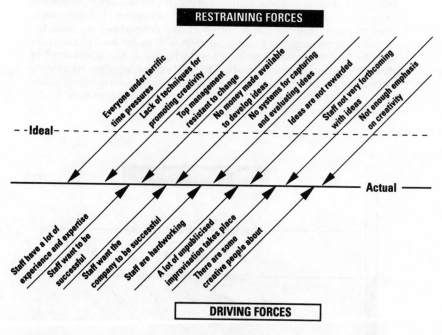

Figure 5   An example of a force-field diagram

As this figure indicates, it is very difficult to add to the driving forces. Such a move could even backfire if, for example, managers tried to make hard-working staff work even harder. The obvious strategy is to reduce the restraining forces. For example:

■ How might some organisational breathing space be provided to enable people to give some thought to innovation?
■ How could the lack of creative-thinking techniques be overcome?

■ How might top management become less resistant to change?
   And so on.

Remember that this is only an example. Not all diagrams will yield the same information, which is, of course, company-specific.

A refinement on force-field analysis is to assign different weights to the various factors according to their relative importance. In Figure 6 the length of the 'force arrows' is proportionate to their degree of influence, with the highest numbers corresponding to the most important factors. The advantage of the weighted-factor approach is that it allows managers to focus on reducing the most important restraining forces rather than the more peripheral ones.

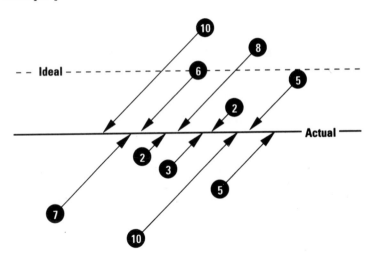

Figure 6   A weighted force-field diagram

It must be recognised, however, that while weighting is an attempt to make the analysis more realistic, it is not meant to be taken too literally. For example, although the restraining and driving forces balance in the diagram, it doesn't follow that their arithmetical sums have to be equal.

Levels of change in organisations

In most cases, assessing a firm's creative climate and how it may be improved will uncover a need for change. Yet organisations are sometimes very difficult to change, having an inbuilt inertia that resists any deviation from the status quo. Anyone faced with the task of improving the climate for creativity in an organisation will not find it easy. Nevertheless, the change agent (as we shall call him or her) can operate at several different levels.

Level 1: Cosmetic change

If the change agent identifies certain symptoms indicating a less-than-ideal organisational climate for creativity, he or she has two options:

- to respond to these symptoms and introduce a change, or
- to regard these symptoms as the tip of an iceberg and try to look deeper to discover what they reveal about the underlying systems in the organisation.

Level 2: Change of system

Assuming the change agent selects the second option, he or she now tries to identify and understand the organisation's systems in terms of how they affect the creative climate. Again this generates two options:

- to change the underlying systems, or
- to dig deeper still and try to identify the underlying values which sustain these inappropriate systems.

Level 3: Change of values

Assuming the second option was taken, the change agent now has to try to identify the deeply held organisational values which, although often unwritten, have a pervasive influence over the way the company conducts its day-to-day business. Having identified these values the change agent will decide that either:

- the current organisational values are consistent with the changes necessary to improve the climate for creativity, or
- the organisational values need to be changed to allow a change in climate to take place.

It is at this level that organisational change is most profound, but at the same time most difficult to achieve. Figure 7 shows how these levels of change might work out in practice.

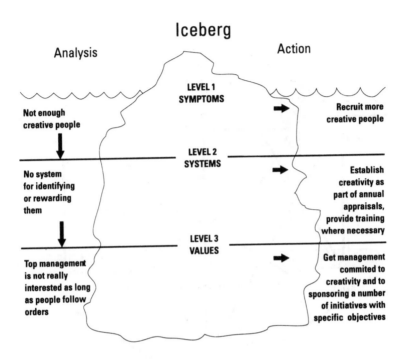

Figure 7   The three levels of organisational change

In this example, the tip of the iceberg could easily elicit the obvious response 'Recruit more creative people.' While this probably would not do any harm, it will not really make much impact if the organisation's management is not overly concerned about creativity. Introducing a process which integrates creativity appraisal and training into the organisation's systems is an action which begins to make impact on the fabric of the organisation. Finally, getting the top management sufficiently commited to creativity to initiate a number of projects themselves is clearly a profound shift that could affect all areas of the company.

Organisational values

The centrality of organisational values is stressed in one influential analysis which concludes that a successful organisation is a framework of interrelated factors whose linchpin, the so-called 'superordinate goals', holds the organisation together and gives it the intellectual stimulus to move in a particular, desired direction (Waterman, Peters and Phillips, 1980). These organisational factors are illustrated in Figure 8.

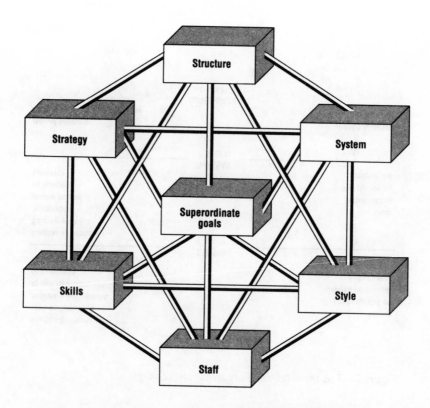

Figure 8   The framework of successful organisations

In everyday parlance 'superordinate goals' are the guiding concepts, values and aspirations, often unwritten, that go beyond a formal, conventional statement of corporate objectives. Successful organisations have superordinate goals which are not only easy to understand at all levels of the organisation, but also well-integrated with the other factors. Often these superordinate goals can be encapsulated in slogans or mottos, such as IBM's 'Customer service and the pursuit of excellence'; McDonald's 'Cleanliness and good service'; G.E.'s 'Progress is our most important product'; and British Airways 'To be the best in everything we do'.

For successful organisations, superordinate goals are not a fancy gimmick but an obsession, something to be worked for at every level of the company, starting at the top. If the top management truly desires the company to become more creative in order to become more innovative, then these two concepts must be integrated into the firm's superordinate goals.

It is almost like adopting a new religion and incorporating it into every aspect of the organisation. This is the most effective - and perhaps the only - way to develop a climate in which creative thinking is 'the right thing to do'.

In turn this means that every other factor in the organisational framework must make a full contribution to the superordinate goals. Each element can have a harmful or beneficial impact on the others and, ultimately, on the ability of the firm to innovate. If this is fully understood, then structure, strategy, skills, style, staff and systems will be developed which are empathetic with the creative process. Unless an organisation sets out to achieve this state of affairs at all levels, any desires it might have to become more creative and innovative are little more than pious hopes.

Effective communication systems

One organisational factor which requires particular attention is the communication system.

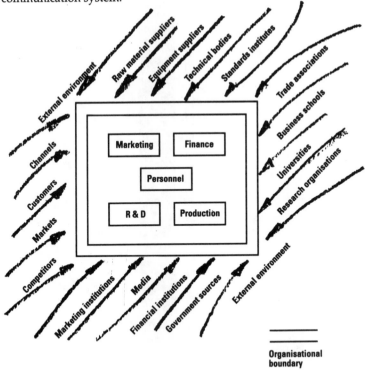

Organisational boundary

Figure 9   The sources and flow of ideas in organisations with no effective system of communication

An organisation's ideas are like gold dust: the more it has, the richer it becomes. Ideas can emerge from every individual, every department and every level of the organisation. Moreover, many valuable ideas can be gleaned from its external environment. Each contact with a customer, supplier, subcontractor, distributor, trade body, financial institution and so on, holds the potential for generating ideas. The problem is how to capture and channel these ideas. If ideas from a number of sources are flying around an organisation at random, with no central place made available to collect them (as in Figure 9), many ideas will be lost.

This is deplorably wasteful. Since statistically something like sixty ideas must be considered and rejected before a successful innovation is found, it is true to say that, in an organisation's search for innovative ideas,

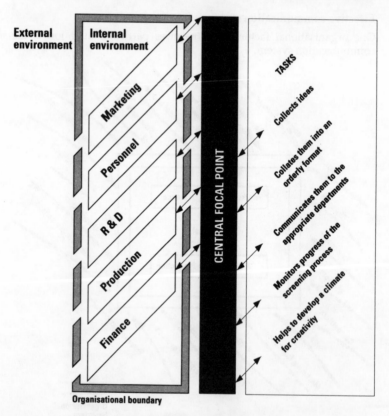

Figure 10 Flow of ideas when an effective communication system exists

quality depends on quantity. Any firm depends on its staff to generate a quantity of ideas. At best, to lose any idea reduces the base from which good ideas are found; at worst, the lost idea may have been the one winner in sixty. Moreover it can be very demoralising - not to say unfair - if, having been encouraged to be more creative, staff do not know how to progress their ideas. Any organisation which truly wants to encourage creativity must have an effective system for collecting and communicating ideas. Such a system is shown in Figure 10 on the preceding page.

In small organisations ideas are relatively easy to communicate informally and directly. As a company grows, the number of its functions or levels also increases and communication tends to become less flexible. Growing companies must recognise this and strive to reverse the erosion of communication that organisational growth can bring. An effective communication system channels the flow of ideas inside departments, between departments and the external environment, and between departments and the central focal point. The central focal point then processes and progresses the ideas in the most appropriate way.

International communication

If a company operates on an international basis, the problem of communication is even more complex. International organisations face the very real risk of the unchannelled flow of ideas illustrated in Figure 9 being reproduced in every operating country. This can be avoided by adopting an extension of the 'idea channelling' concept, which collects and 'distributes' ideas according to two main categories: country and function, as illustrated in Figure 11.

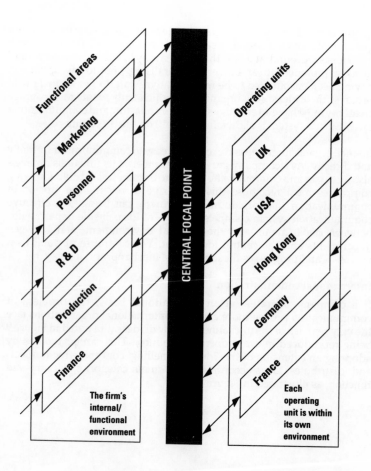

Figure 11 A communication system for a multinational organisation

In this section we have looked at ways of assessing an organisation's prevailing culture or climate with regard to creativity, and discussed some measures for improving it. Once the climate is right, the talents of the creative individuals and groups within the organisation are free to flourish. But who are these people, and how might they be recognised? These issues are examined in the next section.

Creative people are the source of any organisation's creativity and innovation. Yet any discussion of creative people risks running aground on the notion that creative individuals form a separate elite. While it is true that some people are more creative than others, to label individuals as either 'creative' or 'uncreative' is not only invidious but inaccurate, and may in the long run be counter-productive. For one thing, not all creative people are creative all the time, and most people can be creative sometimes. For another, 'creativity' is in the eye of the beholder; whether an individual is regarded as creative or not often depends on the perspective of whoever is doing the assessment. For example, if an employee is expected to work through a problem 'on the back of an envelope', but instead uses a computer to perform the task in an even more ingenious way, he or she may still be judged uncreative if the evaluator is prejudiced in favour of the manual method. (The opposite scenario would also hold true.)

It is in an organisation's interests to recognise and foster the creativity of all its members. If it takes some fifty or sixty ideas to produce one successful innovation, a firm needs as large a pool of ideas as possible from which to select the best. It is a serious mistake to reject ideas (or prevent them being volunteered in the first place) because they originate from 'inappropriate' or unexpected sources, although sadly this happens all too often.

We can all become more creative, and most of us are in fact more creative than we believe. Creativity is largely a self-fulfilling prophesy, as the following figures illustrate.

Each time we work round the positive loop our creativity is affirmed and

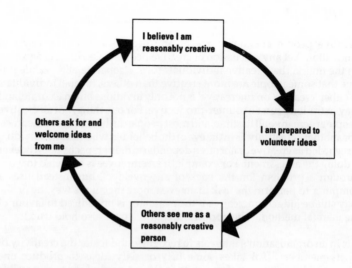

Figure 12 The positive circuit

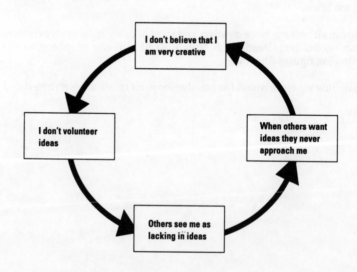

Figure 13 The negative circuit

this strengthens our capability to volunteer ideas. By contrast, experiencing the negative loop only serves to reinforce our own negative self-image and gradually erodes our ability to come forward with ideas. The conclusion is clear: fostering a climate in which creativity can flourish is not only a matter of organisational structure and procedures, it is also a matter of personal outlook. The individuals within an organisation (again, starting with the top levels) must nurture confidence and the willingness to 'have a go' both in themselves and in their colleagues if the organisation's full creative potential is to be tapped.

The Brain and Creativity

It is easier to understand how creativity can be fostered if we understand something of how the brain works. Even now, relatively little is known about the brain, and virtually 90% of what is known has been discovered within the last twenty years. There is still much that remains a mystery, yet certain proven features of brain function shed light on our creative processes.

The human brain, when viewed from above, consists of two hemispheres connected by numerous nerve fibres.

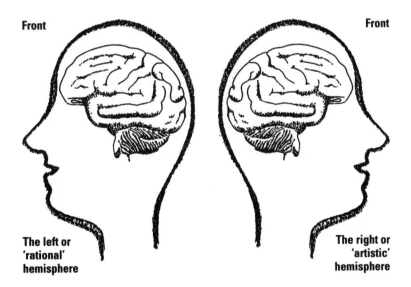

Figure 14 The human brain

The nervous system is connected to the brain in such a way that the right hemisphere controls the functions of the left side of the body and vice versa. (This explains the pattern of paralysis which can occur when a person suffers a stroke or a serious head injury. Damage to the left hemisphere will cause paralysis on the right side of the body.)

By measuring brain activity as a person tackles various tasks, it has been found that each half of the brain deals with different mental activities.

The left hemisphere deals with:
- logic
- language
- numeracy
- analysis
- linear information
- digital thinking
- abstract thinking

The right hemisphere deals with:
- rhythm
- colour
- images
- music
- non-linear information
- shapes
- general creativity

Until fairly recently it was generally held by scientists that the left hemisphere is the major or dominant part of the brain. The most current school of thought, however, suggests that although the functions of the right side of the brain are suppressed or undervalued in most western cultures (just think about school topics and what you need to know to 'get on'), physiologically the two halves ought to be balanced. It is now generally accepted that it is possible to develop the under-utilised half of the brain. Thus accountants and mathematicians ought to be capable of releasing the hidden artistic talent locked away in the right hemispheres of their brains. Equally, artists and daydreamers have the same potential to develop more logical thinking abilities.

It is particularly significant that when people develop the weaker functions of their brainpower, their strong areas are not reduced in any way; instead overall mental performance improves. Einstein is remembered as a scientific genius, and yet he also painted and played the violin competently. Indeed, he claimed that the seed of his theory of relativity first came to him as a 'picture in his mind'. Conversely, we know of artists such as Michelangelo and Leonardo da Vinci whose grasp of engineering was years ahead of their time.

Creativity is not solely the fortunate possession of 'right-brain dominant' people. Many of the creative-thinking techniques provided in Section 5 are designed to stimulate the right hemisphere. With regular exercise it can be brought up to strength in all of us. In practice we all need a well-developed right hemisphere to enable us to generate a wealth of imaginative and unusual ideas. At the same time we need our left hemisphere to sort 'the wheat from the chaff'.

Identifying creative individuals

Although it is recognised that everyone has the potential to think creatively, it is also true that some people's creativity is more highly developed than others', or is combined with certain personality traits which allow it to flourish. On the other hand, some individuals, for whatever reason, seem to have an internal censor forever damping down their own creativity and that of the people around them. In cases where creative problem-solving is required in an organisation (especially as a matter of urgency), obviously it is most efficient to draw upon the talents of the former type of individual. Indeed, the latter type often proves to be a hindrance in situations of creative group work such as the idea-generating exercises described in Section 5.

It is not always easy to identify the most creative people in an organisation. Psychological and psychometric tests tend to be limited to identifying circumstantial signs of likely creativity, rather than creativity itself. Creative people, as we noted earlier, are not creative all the time. Often creativity comes as a sudden, blinding insight, triggered by chance stimuli. Even so, there does seem to be some commonality about the characteristics of creative people. A creative individual will usually demonstrate a few, if not all, of the following qualities.

Conceptual fluency

A creative person can usually generate many ideas in a short time, in response to a given situation. Of course, the most reliable indication of this ability is performance in the workplace, over time. But it also becomes evident in individuals' responses to exercises such as:

- List as many possible uses for a pencil as you can.
- Devise a number of activities that would keep patients entertained in a dentist's waiting-room.
- List ways of reducing litter in public places.
- List names beginning with the letter 'J'.

Mental flexibility

Creative people can easily discard one line of thought and switch to other, loosely-related frames of reference. They can focus on small issues or step back and take in the broad, overall picture. A creative individual can also be something of a juggler and, mentally speaking, keep several balls in the air at the same time.

Originality

This is the ability to give unusual or unexpected answers to questions or problems. Such originality might appear in the guise of creating 'jokes' out of everyday, mundane situations. Alternatively it might manifest as rare and unusual interpretations of ambiguous 'pictures' like the 'inkblot' below.

Figure 15 Finding a number of unusual interpretations of pictures
such as this inkblot indicates a creative mind

Curiosity

Creative people tend to be interested in the world around them, in ideas, events, nature, other people, technology, cultural or leisure pursuits, and so on. As Dr Johnson wrote, 'Curiosity is one of the permanent and certain characteristics of a vigorous intellect.' A wide-ranging and voracious curiosity can be very helpful in allowing individuals to make connections between disparate and seemingly unrelated things - one of the hallmarks of a creative mind.

Suspension of judgement

This is a very important and valuable characteristic in creative team-work. Innovative ideas generally start life as tentative, half-baked notions which could never withstand rigorous analysis. Creative people recognise that seedling ideas need to be protected from harsh, overly-hasty criticism. By not rushing into judgement, creative people allow themselves to play with ideas - those of other people as well as their own - and thus discover their positive aspects as well as their drawbacks. They can therefore make more balanced appraisals which will be further down the creative track than those of their judgemental colleagues.

This quality can be demonstrated in an individual's responses to questions such as:

- What do you think of an idea for producing chess sets with the pieces made out of chocolate?
- What do you think of the idea of getting more people to take their holidays in the UK, rather than abroad?
- What do you think of the idea of motorising the wheelbarrow?
- What do you think of the idea of putting 'governors' on cars so that they can't exceed 50 m.p.h.?

Impulse acceptance

Creative people are more likely than their less creative colleagues to accept bizarre or unorthodox solutions to problems. Because such ideas trigger their imaginations, creative people are more likely to respond impulsively, whereas others would opt for more measured and conventional behaviour. It is difficult to test for this characteristic, but most of us have witnessed it in group discussions at work.

Lack of deference

Highly creative people are more willing to challenge authority than less creative individuals (although not everyone who challenges authority is necessarily creative). It appears that creative people are motivated by the challenge of a problem and find that issues of hierarchical power and authority tend to get in the way.

An individual's attitude to authority might be gauged in several ways:

- Careful assessment of past behaviour.
- Discussions about career history, especially why he or she changed jobs at any particular time. Research indicates that creative people often leave jobs when they perceive them to have become too routine or bounded by bureaucracy.
- Reactions to a case study depicting conflict between a boss and a subordinate. Individuals who question authority are more likely to take the side of the subordinate.

Tolerance

Creative people tend to be very tolerant of other people's ideas. This trait is related to the ability to suspend judgement. It comes into play specifically as a tendency to respond generously and allow other people the freedom to explore and even indulge their own creativity.

Visualisation

Creative individuals often speak in terms of images or mental pictures when trying to describe how they 'see' a problem and its solution. This kind of visual imagination is evidence of an active right hemisphere.

Persistence

Creative people often tend to become intrigued – even obsessed – with a problem and refuse to give up until a solution is found. They will mull over a problem and even seem to be able to set their subconscious minds to work on it while they're asleep or consciously thinking of something else. Inspiration, when it comes, might occur at some odd moment while walking the dog or mowing the lawn, rather than while sitting at a desk at work.

Creativity assessment

The following Creative Traits Assessment Worksheet might prove to be useful in helping to identify the creative people in your organisation. For each individual under consideration, select a 'score' for each trait, where 0 indicates that the quality is completely absent and 10 indicates that it is highly characteristic of the individual. A more balanced assessment may be reached if several people assess each individual independently and the various 'scores' for each person are averaged.

Creative Traits Assessment Worksheet

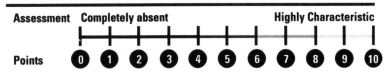

Assessment	Completely absent								Highly Characteristic		
Points	0	1	2	3	4	5	6	7	8	9	10

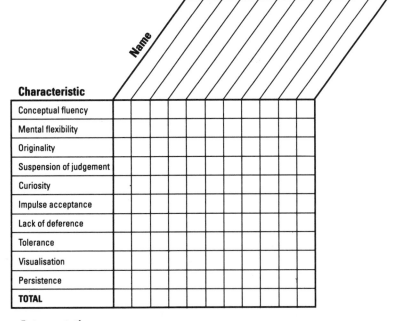

Characteristic	Name										
Conceptual fluency											
Mental flexibility											
Originality											
Suspension of judgement											
Curiosity											
Impulse acceptance											
Lack of deference											
Tolerance											
Visualisation											
Persistence											
TOTAL											

Interpretation

over 75	Exceptionally creative, a rare species
62 - 75	Very creative, a valuable asset
50 - 61	Useful to have around during creativity work
37 - 49	An acceptable average
25 - 36	Needs a lot of encouragement and development
under 25	Not very creative, could block creative work groups

By definition, an organisation involves a group of individuals working together towards common goals. Teamwork is thus intrinsic to organisations, and should be incorporated in their pursuit of creativity and innovation no less than in any other aspect of their operations. Apart from the fact that group work is unavoidable in all but the smallest firms, there is one important reason why creative teamwork is positively desirable: more ideas are produced when individuals work together in a group than when the same individuals work alone. Provided creativity groups are carefully selected and skilfully led, the interplay between the various members' imaginations and range of experience can generate not only more ideas, but ideas of greater quality.

Generally each organisation tailors its groups to suit its own, company-specific needs. As we saw in Section 1, creativity itself can be categorised as either normative (i.e. focused on a specific problem) or exploratory (i.e. freewheeling, unfocused and opportunity-seeking). Each of the following types of creative group can be orientated towards either normative or exploratory creativity. A group's orientation can shift from one focus to the other as the need arises.

Ad hoc creative groups

By far the most common type of creative group in most organisations is the ad hoc group, formed either within a specific department or function or interdepartmentally, to work on specific problems or identify opportunities, as the need arises. Such groups tend to function best when they have no fewer than six and no more than twelve participants, although larger groups can be broken down into subgroups with good results. Most of the creativity techniques described in Section 5 are useful in ad hoc creative groups.

In addition to the temporary, ad hoc type of creative group, there are also two broad categories of more permanent creative group:

- Creativity circles and
- Think Tanks.

Creativity circles

Creativity circles are small, voluntary groups of employees performing similar work in an organisation, who meet regularly to discuss problems and foment ideas. Such groups have evolved from the Quality Circle movement which has swept Japanese industry in the past several decades. Generally, at the operational level these groups are orientated towards normative creativity; at the management and strategic levels they may focus on either normative or exploratory creativity.

Creativity circles are usually, but not necessarily, led by participants who hold supervisory or senior positions, but the leader's role is more that of facilitator than director. The groups are usually no larger than a dozen individuals. Participants meet regularly (often weekly) in the firm's time, using techniques such as those described in Section 5 to identify, analyse and solve work-related problems (in the case of normative work), or pinpoint likely opportunities (in the case of exploratory work). They often make formal presentations of their findings to the more senior levels of the organisation and implement their approved recommendations themselves as part of the group's normal operation.

If creativity circles are taken seriously by top management and given the resources they need to function effectively (including adequate training for both group leaders and members), they can bring a number of advantages to an organisation:

- the financial benefits and competitive edge associated with innovative products, working practices, marketing techniques and the like
- higher morale among employees
- improved communication within the organisation
- greater commitment to organisational goals
- lower absenteeism
- a more positive corporate image.

Think Tanks

In contrast to the self-selecting, inclusive nature of creativity circles, Think Tanks tend to be appointive and exclusive. Think Tanks are generally set up by large organisations - governments, political parties, companies, pressure groups, industrial bodies and the like - to provide fresh, creative, independent and far-sighted solutions to the issues upon which they have been invited to reflect. Usually these issues are matters of future strategy and direction which are outside the organisation's normal, day-to-day operations.

To be successful, Think Tanks must have very clearly defined, specific objectives. The membership of such groups must be carefully selected both on the basis of each participant's compatibility with the group's aims (technical expertise, relevant experience and so on) and on his or her personal suitability in terms of creativity, commitment, positive attitude to teamwork, and so on. As with most creative groups, Think Tanks function most effectively when they are composed of six to twelve members. It is crucial that Think Tanks have effective and skilful leaders well-versed both in creativity exercises and in the techniques of directing and facilitating group work. Such groups usually meet on a monthly basis, and members are asked to take on the extra responsibility associated with their participation in the Think Tank in addition to their usual, day-to-day responsibilities in the organisation.

The objectives and operations of a Think Tank must have the full support of the organisation's senior management, and the group must not be saddled with an untenably difficult 'political' position within the organisation (such as having to please too many masters, having insufficient authority to gather information essential to its mission, and the like). It is also vital that the Think Tank is not seen as an elitist clique within the organisation, but rather that its objectives and contributions are well understood and supported. This requires considerable efforts of communication and public relations on the part of the group and, again, active, enthusiastic support for these efforts on the part of senior management. Techniques for the optimal functioning of Think Tanks are discussed in Section 5.

If a Think Tank is given optimal resources and conditions to function effectively, it can bring the following benefits to an organisation:

■ increased innovation, with all its associated competitive advantages
■ an objective, considered and creative vision of the organisation's future role, goals and strategies, and the confidence and organisational focus which this engenders
■ a proactive, rather than reactive, emphasis within the organisation
■ the ability to shape the future developments or thinking of the firm

(For fuller discussions of creativity circles, Think Tanks and creative groups in general, see Majaro, *The Creative Gap*, 1988.)

How creative are you?

The following exercises are designed to explore the extent to which you think laterally and are prepared to look for solutions outside the obvious search area. They do not represent a scientific method of assessment and should not be taken literally as evidence of creative prowess or the lack thereof.

---

1 **Matchsticks**

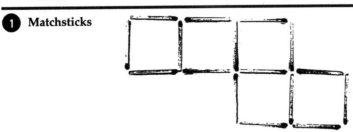

Convert the above layout of matchsticks to four equal-sized squares by repositioning just two of the matchsticks. All the matchsticks are used in the solution.

---

2 **Nine-dots puzzle**

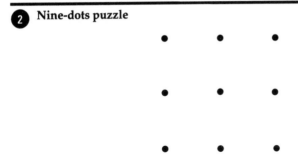

Join up the nine dots with four straight, continuously-drawn lines – in other words, without lifting your pencil off the paper.

More difficult version
Join all the dots with a single straight line. If you solve this you are being very creative.

3 **Letter progression**

Continue and explain the following progression of letters.

A	EF	HI	–	–	–
BCD	G	J	–	–

4 **Numeric progression**

Continue and explain the following progression of numbers.

3 1 2 8 3 1 3 0 – – – – – – – – –

5 **The golf course**

A new golf course has just been opened and the par scores for the first nine holes are as follows:

3 3 5 4 4 3 5 5 4

What 'rule' has the course architect used to arrive at this layout?

6 **The four trees**

Four trees have been bought from a garden centre. Your task is to plant them in such a way that they are equidistant from each other at the points where the trunks meet the ground.

7 Shapes

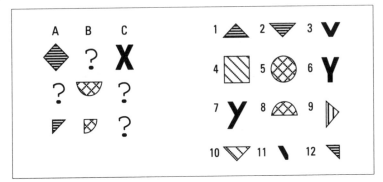

Complete the pattern in each of the left-hand columns above by choosing four shapes from the selection on the right.

8 The tennis tournament

The secretary of the local tennis club receives 55 entries for the Gentlemen's Singles Tournament, an annual event which is organised on a knock-out basis. His first concern is to establish how many matches will have to be played to complete the tournament, so that he can reserve enough court time.

What is the answer?

9 The staircase

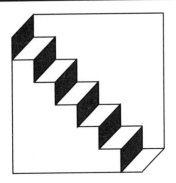

Do you see the staircase from above or below?

10 **The treasure box**

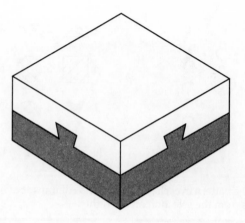

The treasure box is made of two halves dovetailed together as shown. Can you visualise a way in which the two halves can be separated without damaging the structure of the dovetails?

Solutions

1 **Matchsticks**

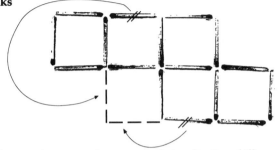

This puzzles requires a certain amount of visualisation skill.

2 **Nine-dots puzzle**

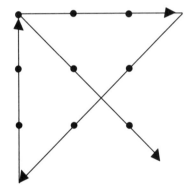

This puzzle requires lateral thinking to escape the trap of operating only within the confines of the square described by the nine dots.

More difficult version

Two solutions are known at present:
- Use a broad brush which covers all nine dots at a stroke.
- Imagine a line going through the top row of dots at a very slight angle, which goes right round the world and passes first through the middle row then, after another circumference of the globe, through the bottom row.

If you thought of a third solution, you are truly a genius.

3 Letter progression

The progression should finish up thus:

A	EF	HI	KLMN	T	VWXYZ
BCD	G	J	OPQRS	U	

The letters above the line are composed only of straight lines; those below have curves.

This solution requires good observation skills and a flexible mind.

---

4 Numeric progression

Taken in pairs, the numbers indicate the sequence of the number of days of the month. Thus January = 31, February = 28, March = 31, and so on.

Anyone solving this puzzle without prompting demonstrates a high level of creativity and lateral thinking.

---

5 The golf course

The 'rule' behind the course design is that the par score equates to the number of letters of the hole number. Thus ONE = par 3, TWO = par 3, THREE = par 5, and so on.

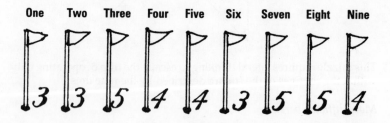

Only an extremely flexible mind is likely to spot this without prompting.

6 **The four trees**

The puzzle is impossible to solve if the ground is considered flat. The only solutions are:

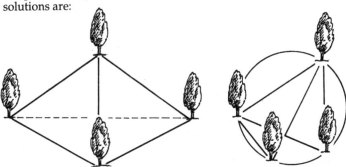

One tree is planted either on a hill or in a dell, so that the base of its trunk is diagonally equidistant from those of the other three trees, which are planted at equal distances from each other in the same plane.

7 **Shapes**

The progression of the shapes is 'whole figure' in the top row, 'half figure' in the middle row and 'quarter figure' in the bottom row. Thus:

- Shape 2 completes the A column.
- Shape 5 completes the B column.
- Shapes 3 and 11 complete the C column.

Again, good observing skills and a flexible mind are required to solve this puzzle.

8 **The tennis tournament**

The temptation here is to work out the number of matches on a pyramid basis, according to an arithmetical progression, i.e. one final, two semi-finals, four quarter-finals and so on. However, because this is a knock-out tournament, there can only be one winner; everybody else must lose. Thus with an entry of 55 players, 54 matches must be played in order to get 54 losers.

Again, this puzzle requires attentiveness and good lateral thinking.

9 **The staircase**

In fact the staircase can be seen from both above and below. Those who can see both 'pictures' simultaneously demonstrate strong observing skills and mental flexibility.

10 **Treasure box**

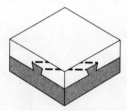

One possible solution would be to slide the two pieces of the puzzle apart diagonally as shown. As with most of the other puzzles, the solution here is found by abandoning the obvious and looking at things from a new perspective.

The techniques designed to promote creativity and innovation fall into two major categories:

- **diagnostic techniques and**
- **idea-generating techniques.**

These two types of technique – and the two separate phases of problem-solving to which they relate – are equally important. Diagnostic techniques, as the term implies, tend to be more analytical, and idea-generating techniques more strictly 'creative', although the creativity involved in the diagnostic work should not be underestimated.

(For fuller information on the creativity techniques discussed in this section, see Majaro, 1988).

Diagnostic techniques
Before creative thinking is undertaken to solve a problem or identify an opportunity, both the details and the importance of the project must be identified. Otherwise it will be unclear what the true nature of the task really is, or indeed whether it is even worth bothering about. It is essential to be able to state a problem or issue clearly, to marshall all the relevant facts known about it, and to determine what priority it holds for the organisation.

If this phase of the process is ignored, the search for solutions becomes overly vague and can end up being a futile waste of time. Sheer common sense dictates that solutions to a problem cannot be found if no one knows what the problem is, yet it can sometimes be tempting to dispense with the necessary spadework involved in this preliminary phase of problem-solving and plunge straight into the idea-generating stage. This temptation should be resisted, however, because:

- Successful creative solutions to problems depend on a specific and detailed understanding of the issues involved.
- If this preliminary analytical work is neglected, any solutions found are likely to be overly-general or inappropriate.
- Group idea-generating techniques can founder on points of information.
- Unsuccesful solutions are discouraging and can erode commitment and generate hostility and scepticism within the organisation towards attempts to promote creativity and innovation.
- Unsuccessful solutions are a waste of time and money.

The following exercises are designed to provide a systematic range of methods for identifying and defining problems and for assigning priorities to them.

Priority ranking of problems

Facing problems is a bit like waiting for a bus. Nothing much happens for a while, then a lot of them arrive at more or less the same time. It is therefore necessary to have a method of prioritising problems in order to know which ones will be the most worthwhile investments of time and energy. The form below can be used for this purpose.

List the various problems under consideration as headings to the vertical columns. Then assess each problem in terms of the questions listed down the page, according to the following system of scoring. The higher the total score the greater the problem's priority. Add any relevant remarks in the 'User's comments' column.

Your Answer	Irrelevant	Worth noting	Fairly important	Important	Extremely important
Points	0	1	2	3	4

Problems	1	2	3	4	5	6	7	User's Comments
Is the problem considered large?								
Does it involve the company in losses or added costs?								
Is a solution urgently required?								
Will customers appreciate the removal or solution of this problem?								
Will the company's image be enhanced?								
Will morale improve inside the firm?								
TOTAL								

Fact finding: - diagnostic checklists

Fact-finding is an important element of the diagnostic stage of problem-solving. It allows you to gather all known data about the problem under consideration and to identify unknown data which must be obtained before the problem can be fully understood. This has two possible benefits:

■ Sometimes simply marshalling the relevant facts about an issue reveals the best solution without any further procedures being necessary.

■ Focusing on the problem in an informed way stimulates the mental processes and generates more creative ideas than would be possible if the individual or group was less well-informed on the subject.

The following list of questions will help you with your fact-finding. Add any remarks or further questions which you feel are useful in the 'User's comments' column.

What?	User's comments
What is the total situation of which this problem is part? What is the size of the problem (large, medium or small)? What will happen if no action is taken? What will happen if the solution is delayed? Into what parts can the problem be divided? What other problems relate to this problem?	

Why?	
Why did the problem occur in the first place? Why was the problem not recognised earlier? Why did no one try to solve the problem earlier?	

When?	
When was the problem first noticed? Is the time when the problem appeared significant? Is there any seasonal or cyclic pattern to the occurrence of the problem?	

How?	User's comments

How did the problem come to be recognised?
How does the problem affect the company's performance?
How (if it is recurring) was it dealt with before?
How was it prevented from occurring or recurring in the past?

Where?

Is the problem confined to only one part of the organisation?
Is the problem confined to only one part of the world/country/region/market/distribution outlet?
If the answer to the question above is 'Yes' is this significant?

Who?

Who first identified the existence of the problem?
Who was responsible for the problem occurring?
Who could be made responsible for solving it?
Who is the person (or what is the department or market segment) worst affected by the continued existence of the problem?
Who is the person (or what is the department or market segment) most likely to benefit from a solution to the problem?
Who should be consulted in order to solve the problem?

Brain patterns

Often a problem and its context can be fruitfully explored through a technique designed to release the mind from the constraints of rigid linear and sequential patterns of thinking and exploit the way it actually generates thoughts. Works by Tony Buzan (*Use Your Head*) and others have provided evidence that the brain doesn't naturally function in a linear manner. Instead the mind operates in multidimensional, non-linear ways. The idea behind the 'brain patterns' approach is to let the mind function as it does naturally — that is, randomly and haphazardly — without the constraints of being forced to order information sequentially.

This is how the idea works in practice. Suppose you were considering the problem of reducing production costs.

Step 1 In the centre of a blank sheet of paper, write down the problem and draw a circle around it.

User's comments

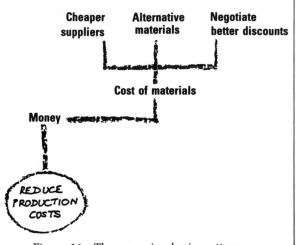

Figure 15 The starting point for a brain-pattern exercise

Step 2 What thoughts enter your mind as you look at this?
Suppose 'money' is your first thought.
List this and each new idea that develops from it as you let your mind explore this issue. Speed is of the essence here; your brain can operate more quickly than you can write, so don't stop to analyse anything, just write it down.

Figure 16   The emerging brain pattern

There is no right or wrong in this process, you are just letting your mind wander where it will.

Step When one strand of thought is exhausted, go back to the centre and unravel another one.

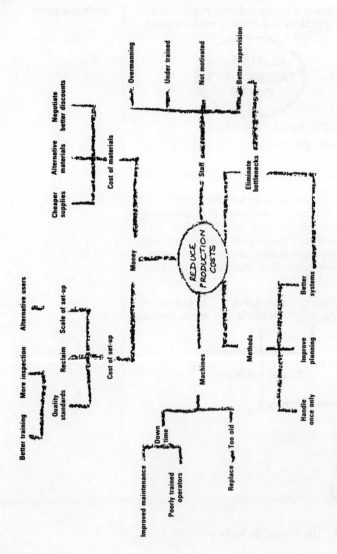

Figure 17 An example of a completed 'brain pattern

Figure 17 shows a completed brain pattern, for this example.
Initially, brain patterns should take only a few minutes to produce.
You can often see ways of adding to a 'completed' pattern, however, if
you go back to it later.

 Step

Once the brain pattern is finished to your
satisfaction, it may be used as a starting point
for a more analytical type of thinking in which
themes and linkages among the various
elements of the pattern are identified and
perhaps prioritised.

User's comments

This technique can be used either by an
individual or a group to explore any multidimensional problem. The key to using this
approach is to get the ideas out first, and only
then to impose a structure on them.

The fishbone diagram

The Fishbone Diagram is a tool to facilitate the analysis of a problem's
cause and effect, so that the real root of the problem – rather than
merely its symptoms – may be identified and addressed. The diagram
was developed by Professor Kaoru Ishikawa of Tokyo University. His
choice of name for this technique will become obvious as the diagram is
explained. Although it may be used by individuals, this approach is
perhaps most productive when undertaken by a group.

Step

Draw a straight line across a piece of paper
with a circle at one end. Inside the circle write
the problem under discussion. This in effect is
the head and the spine of the 'fish' as the
following illustration shows.

User's comments

Figure 18   The first stage of the fishbone diagram: the problem

Step 1 Next draw stems at about 45° along the spine. These stems represent every likely cause of the problem that the group can think of, which in turn are written inside circles at the ends of the stems. The stems should be drawn long enough to leave space for sub-stems to be drawn in-between them and the spine.

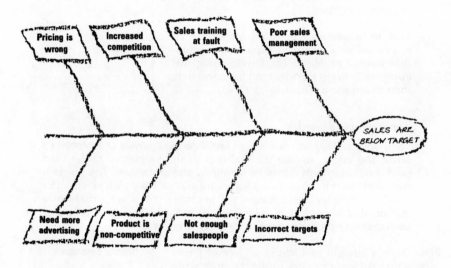

Figure 19   The second stage of the fishbone diagram: the problem and its likely causes

Step 2 Each stem is examined in turn and further branches are added to represent sub-issues that have a bearing on any particular cause. It does not matter if a particular issue appears more than once, indeed, it might be highly significant if it does. Gradually the whole fishbone is built up as in Figure 20. Recurring or especially important issues can be identified with asterisks or coloured markers.

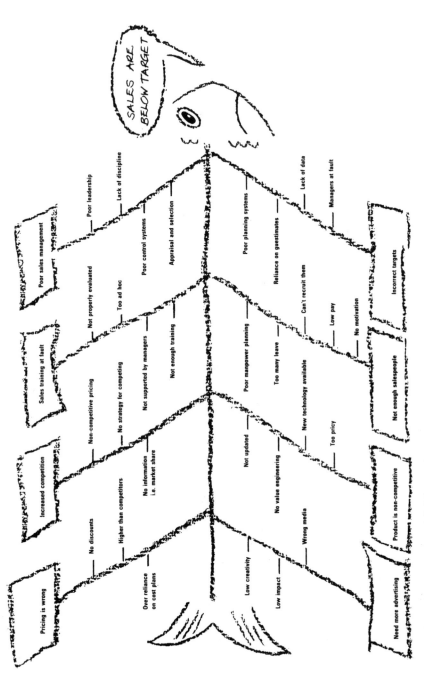

Figure 20   The completed fishbone diagram

A 'Fishbone Diagram' can be built up over a number of sessions — indeed, this can bring certain benefits:

- Fresh ideas can occur to group members during the intervals between sessions.
- Members of the group forget who contributed which idea and can therefore address the diagram without feeling worried about 'treading on other people's toes'.
- The team have a visual stimulus which will enable them to reflect on the problem at odd hours, perhaps even in their sleep.

Step 4 When the diagram is considered to be fully developed, or 'cooked' as Ishikawa likes to call it, the group discusses each stem and sub-stem in detail. Its objective is to identify the main issues that will have to be resolved in order to make impact on the original problem, and to rank these issues in order of priority. (The Priority Ranking Worksheet may be used to help with this process.)

The Fishbone Diagram is a simple yet logical method of breaking a problem down into its constituent parts. In an organisational context it provides a number of benefits which make it a very valuable tool for managers.

- It encourages all team members to explore the many different aspects of a problem before rushing in with solutions.
- It helps to show the relationships and relative importance of the component parts of a problem – something which is often overlooked.
- It launches the creative process, in that it focuses people's minds on a problem in a non-judgemental and non-attributive manner.
- It provides a systematic method for dealing with a problem, thus keeping everyone on track.
- It forces people to take a broad view, because the fishbone isn't 'cooked' until a wide range of information is made available.

User's comments

■ Because of the thoroughness of this approach, it helps to produce workable solutions to which people are committed.

The why - why diagram

This is a variation on the same theme as the Fishbone Diagram. Again, its purpose is to penetrate to the roots of a problem in a systematic way. While, like the Fishbone Diagram, it can be employed by an individual, this technique is much more successful if a group work at developing the diagram. This is what happens in a typical group setting.

Step The problem as it has been presented to the group is written on a flip-chart or blackboard.

User's comments

Step The group is now asked to submit ideas as to the reasons *why* what is written on the board is in fact a problem. In this way, just by asking the question 'Why?' in a persistent and enquiring manner, a whole range of underlying issues is uncovered.

Step Each underlying issue and its contributory factor(s) are challenged with the question 'Why?' until each strand of the problem is teased out as far as possible.

Step 4 When the Why-Why Diagram is complete, the problem-solving group should be in a much stronger position to understand the exact nature of the problem and its underlying causes. By analysing the Why-Why Diagram, the group should be able to restate the real problem in terms of its root causes – and by doing so, be well on the way to coming up with a good solution.

The Why-Why method brings with it most of the benefits attributed to the Fishbone Diagram. In particular, it encourages participants to think in an expansive, divergent way, rather than getting bogged down too early in any fixed direction of thought.

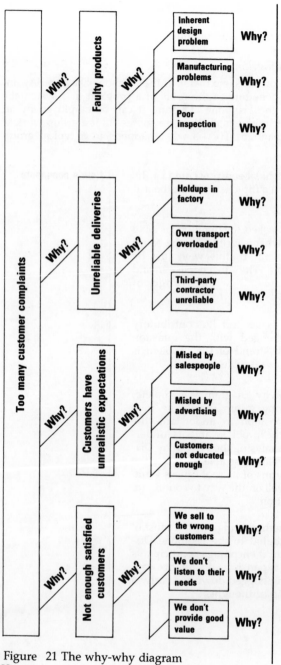

User's comments

Figure 21 The why-why diagram

Idea-generating techniques	**User's comments**

After the diagnostic stage has been satisfactorily concluded, the following idea-generating techniques may be used to proceed with the problem-solving or opportunity-seeking process:

- attribute listing
- brainstorming
- metaphorical analogy
- morphological analysis
- scenario writing and scenario day-dreaming
- trigger sessions
- wildest idea sessions.

Generally these techniques are most appropriate for use by creative groups.

In addition to describing these idea-generating techniques, this section also contains a detailed discussion of how to implement two quite different (but not mutually exclusive) methods for promoting creativity and innovation in an organisation:

- suggestion schemes and
- Think Tanks.

Attribute listing

This is a simple technique which can be used with some success if the problem involves finding ways to improve an existing product or service. It entails listing the current features or attributes of the product and exploring ways in which each one could be improved. Suppose a company wanted to come up with some ideas for a better food whisk.

Step 1 The first step would be to list the attributes of their existing model, for example:

User's comments

- made of stainless steel
- wooden handles
- hand-operated
- variable speed
- can be used anywhere
- needs two hands to use.

(There are many other types of attributes, including more technical ones, which could be listed.)

Step 2
Each of these attributes is then considered in turn and questions are asked about the ways in which it might be improved, for example:

Wooden handles
- Could they be in other materials?
- Should they have finger grooves?
- Should they be in a range of colours?
- Should they be of an entirely different design?

Needs two hands to use
- Could it be made for one-handed use, say for disabled people?
- Might a one-handed model involve pump action?
- Might it need to be motorised?

And so on. As many questions as possible are generated for each attribute.

Step 3
All the best ideas from Step 2 are taken forward for evaluation.

Attribute listing may be used on its own or as one means of generating the many options considered in morphological analysis, a technique discussed later in this section.

Brainstorming

Brainstorming is an idea-generating technique developed by Alex Osborn in the early 1950s (Osborn, 1963). He was convinced that people can be more creative if only they stop being so critical of their ideas. In his view, ideas are generated most successfully in a relaxed and judgement-free atmosphere which enables people to 'take the brakes off'. Brainstorming is based on the belief that the collective brain-power of a group of people can outperform that of an individual when it comes to creative problem-solving or generating exploratory ideas. Only after a large number of ideas has been accumulated should they be subjected to critical examination.

Facilities

A brainstorming session should be conducted in a suitably-sized room, neither so small as to crowd the participants or so large as to make them feel too far away from each other. It should be free from outside interruptions, sufficiently warm, well-ventilated and well-lit, and provided with comfortable chairs.

User's comments

User's comments

There must be a flip-chart or the equivalent available. Seating should be arranged so that the participants have maximum opportunity to interact; a circle is probably best for this, or a semi-circle facing the flip-chart. There is no need to sit round a table – indeed sometimes furniture can be a barrier to interaction.

User's comments

Number of participants

There is no magic number, but groups of about 8–10 people seem to work very well. Too large and the group becomes unwieldy, too small and the prospect for creative interaction is reduced.

Roles

There are two key roles in any brainstorming group:

■ *Leader.* This person acts as chairman; his or her prime role is to organise, stimulate and control the proceedings. Often gentler, soft-spoken, non-authoritarian figures play this role more effectively than their more domineering and aggressive counterparts. There is no reason why the leadership role should not rotate within the brainstorming group from one session to another.
■ *Scribe.* This person records all the ideas that are generated. He or she needs to be able to write on vertical surfaces very quickly and clearly. Because ideas can be thrown at the scribe rapidly and in great numbers, an ability to paraphrase them without losing their meaning can be a valuable asset.

Osborn advocated that the rest of the group should be made up as follows:
■ *Core members.* These should constitute half the group and should be people who have shown:
□ an aptitude for contributing a large number of ideas
□ a high degree of tolerance of other people's ideas
□ a high level of conceptual fluency.

89

In large organisations there can be an advantage in drawing these people from different departments, since the differences in their backgrounds and experience can contribute to the cross-fertilisation of ideas.

- ■ *Guest members.* These participants may be invited for a single meeting, or be listed on a roster to attend brainstorming sessions intermittently. The advantages of including guest members are:
- ☐ The group doesn't become too predictable, stale and inward-looking
- ☐ Guests can become 'missionaries' to spread the word to the 'unconverted' in their departments of the organisation
- ☐ Being involved can reduce a guest's scepticism about brainstorming.
  There are two provisos, however:
- ☐ Guests should not be completely negative about brainstorming, otherwise they will inhibit the process.
- ☐ Guests should be of similar status to the other participants so that issues of deference or seniority do not inhibit the creative process. In informal organisations, where the position and status of individuals does not create intimidating situations, this point can be ignored.

Procedure

Step 1 *Explain the technique.* Ensure that everyone present understands the 'rules', which are:

- ■ The aim of the session is to generate as many ideas as possible.
- ■ This involves the need to suspend judgement on any idea put forward (the evaluation of ideas will come later).
- ■ For the session to be effective, people must be willing to 'free-wheel' and disclose any ideas they have, regardless of how silly or outrageous they might seem at the time.
- ■ Out of quantity will come quality.

Step 2 *Warm-up exercise.* This is the mental equivalent of the limbering-up routine an athlete goes through before a race. The objective is to get people relaxed and in the right frame of mind. Here are some suggestions for conducting a warm-up:

- Use games, puzzles or quizzes similar to the ones at the end of Section 4.
- Get each person to volunteer a funny story.
- Introduce a 'dummy' brainstorming exercise, for example, new uses for a paperclip or any other everyday object such as a felt-tipped pen, an ashtray or a coin.

The warm-up session should take as long as necessary to serve its purpose. However, since time is always a valuable commodity, a notional target of about 20–30 minutes should be set for the warm-up.

Step 3 *Debrief of the warm-up.* Check how people felt about the session and find out if there were any points which could be carried over into the main session to make it more effective.

Step 4 *Define the task.* Often participants will not be entirely clear about the task they are to address. For example, 'improving communications' could be construed by some as a problem with the telephone system, by others as producing better written reports and memos, by still others as the need for more effective meetings. Consensus about the task to be tackled is important because everyone working to the same end improves the likelihood of a successful session.

Use techniques like the Fishbone Diagram or the Why-Why Diagram: these will help to bring the real task into focus. Such techniques build on the warm-up session and serve to get people's brains into higher gear. When the problem to be addressed has been satisfactorily identified and defined, write the agreed task on a flip-chart or blackboard so that it is a constant, visible reminder to the group.

User's comments

91

Step **5** *Brainstorming.* The group is now encouraged to provide as many ideas as possible which could make impact on the problem or task under consideration. These should be listed on a flip-chart or the equivalent. All ideas should be visible, because they provide stimulus for new ideas.

A notional target to aim for is 150 ideas (which an experienced group can achieve in about 20 minutes). If progress is slow, have a break and see if that helps, or take time out and have another warm-up session. It is important that the leader shows patience with an inexperienced or slow-moving group so as not to discourage them and lose their potentially valuable ideas.

Step **6** *After the brainstorming session.* The creativity of participants may be so highly charged that they continue to generate ideas for several hours or even days after the brainstorming session. It is important to invite them to submit any new ideas which occur to them later to the scribe or leader. The final list of ideas should then be typed, with each idea numbered according to when it was generated in the session. (This makes evaluation easier.)

It is useful to have the list triple-spaced so that comments can be attached later. The list is now ready to be circulated and evaluated, using one or several of the screening techniques discussed in Section 6.

User's comments

Suitable topics for brainstorming

As a general rule, simple or easily-defined problems are more suitable for brainstorming than complex or multi-faceted ones. Topics or problems for which data and knowledge are available are more suitable than those about which little information can be obtained.

Trouble-shooting problems are ideal for brainstorming, for example, 'how to reduce downtime on No. 2 production line, or 'how to reduce shop-lifting in our store. In addition, any situation calling for a large number of disparate ideas is especially suitable, for instance, identifying new product concepts, new market/segment concepts, names for brands, products or companies, themes for conferences or exhibitions and so on.

Finally, the will to solve the problem must exist among those responsible for it in order to justify it as a topic for a brainstorming session.

Unsuitable topics for brainstorming

Besides topics which fail to meet the criteria described above, the following subjects are inappropriate for brainstorming sessions:

- problems which have only one or very few answers, for example, 'Should we build our new plant in the Midlands or the North-East?'
- problems which need a higher authority for ajudication, for example, 'How can we change the corporate objectives of our parent company?'
- problems which require technical or professional expertise beyond the capability of the members of the brainstorming group.

User's comments

Metaphorical analogy

The underlying principle of this technique is to draw an analogy between a problem for which one does not have a solution, and a comparable problem from a totally different sphere of activity for which an answer does exist. For example, suppose an organisation felt that its management development programme was not paying dividends; managers of the right calibre were not emerging even after all their training and development.

What might be an appropriate analogy for this situation? The activities of gardeners who grow prize-winning flowers might be examined for lessons the organisation could apply in its management training programme. After all, gardeners are attempting to produce winners too, just as the company hopes to do. What can the organisation learn from the example of the gardener?

Here is how the analogy might be developed.

Gardener	Company Management Development
Prepares the ground well and takes into account the suitability of the site in which the seeds will be sown	What might a company learn from this? What is the company equivalent of 'preparing the soil'? Are certain areas more suitable for management training than others?
Selects prize-winning seeds	Is the company actually selecting the right people for development? How might selection be improved?
Sows the seeds and protects them from pests and frosts, while keeping them fed and watered	What are the management equivalents of pests and frosts? What is the best way of 'feeding and watering' developing managers?
Once the shoots begin to show, the weaker ones are weeded out to leave space for the healthier plants	What does this mean in management–development terms? How might this weeding-out process be accomplished in a positive way?

Care continues and the growing plant is tied to a stake for support	What support (e.g. regular counselling) is given to the 'growing' manager? Is a mentor provided? Are there other possible methods of support?
Finally the gardener exhibits the flowers before the judges and is awarded a rosette and certificate to commemorate his or her success	What is the equivalent of the exhibition for the 'fully grown' manager: an exam? A difficult assignment? What else could it be? How can the company be sure it has produced a prize-winner? Who are the judges? What are the prizes? Who receives them – the 'flower' or the 'gardener'?

By studying the prize-winning gardener, the organisation finds a whole range of interesting questions about management development beginning to emerge. One or two of these questions might point to the reasons why the company doesn't produce 'prize-winning' managers. Once the right questions have been identified, it is possible to come up with the right answers.

Analogies are all around us if we care to look.

User's comments

Possible sources of useful analogies include:

- the natural world
- the animal kingdom
- other human cultures and civilisations, past and present
- other industries
- the sciences: chemistry, physics, geology and so on
- the arts and crafts: music, dance, cinema, weaving, woodworking and so on
- sport
- leisure activities.

Often the simplest analogies prove to be the most fruitful.

Metaphorical analogy is a relatively simple technique to use and yet it can often provide some blinding insights into how to overcome seemingly intractable problems. The facilities, number of participants, and facilitators' roles (leader and scribe) are similar to those described for a brainstorming session.

Visual metaphorical analogy

It is often said that one picture is worth a thousand words. Visual metaphorical analogy takes advantage of this by using pictures rather than words to identify the root cause of a problem and the possible creative solutions to it.

The theory behind this approach is that a problem is both something we *know* and something we *feel;* we have an emotional as well as a rational response to it. Sometimes clues to the problem's solution are hidden in our feelings about it. Feelings are not always easy to communicate in words, however, and often pictures can be far more expressive and provide more accurate 'information' about the issue than words can. Artistic skill is not required to use this approach. Drawing of any kind is simply another way of expressing oneself, and one that is more closely connected to the creative right hemisphere of the brain.

Facilities

User's comments

The arrangements for a group session of visual metaphorical analogy are generally similar to those for a brainstorming session, with the addition of a pad of unlined paper and a supply of pencils and coloured markers for each participant. A writing surface of some description (table, desk, clipboard, etc.) should also be provided for each member of the group.

Step 1 *Drawing the problem.* Each participant is asked to draw a picture of what they perceive the problem under consideration to be. Artistic quality is irrelevant; for example, people can be drawn as pin-figures, or indeed, because this is the world of analogy, they might even be drawn as trees or buildings. The use of coloured pencils or markers can often make the pictures more dramatic. However, words should not be used in the pictures unless absolutely necessary.

Step *Drawing the solution.* Each person is then invited to draw a picture of how he or she would like to see the situation look *if the problem had been solved.*

Step *Individual interpretation.* When the pictures have been completed, each person is asked to make a note of how his or her 'solution' picture differs from the 'problem' picture. Having noted all the changes, each participant should then interpret these into analogous steps which could be taken to solve the problem in real life. (This should be done silently, on paper, so as not to influence the following group discussion of the pictures.)

Step *Group interpretation.* Each person displays his or her 'problem' picture for the rest of the group to interpret. Often, quite by chance, some exciting nuances of the problem are uncovered by this 'translation' process.

The same procedure is followed for each of the 'solution' pictures.

Step *Discussing solutions.* In the final phase of the exercise, the group discusses and collates each participant's recommended steps for reaching a solution to the problem. These generally boil down to two or three definite measures that can be implemented to resolve the problem.

This technique can also be used by individual but will lack the stimulus to creativity that a group can provide.

Unsuitable topics for metaphorical analogy

Brainstorming is a good way to identify possible analogies to the problem under consideration. It would be a rare problem indeed which defied all attempts to match it to any analogous situation. However, if this proves to be the case – or if the chosen analogy is too remote or contrived – it might be more productive to seek a solution using other idea-generating techniques.

Morphological analysis

This complicated-sounding term is a most valuable technique for generating a large number of ideas in a short time. It originated in the complex technological world of astrophysics and rocket research in the 1940s and was the work of Fritz Zwicky a Swiss astronomer. It is only in recent years that Zwicky's analytical technique has emerged from the depths of research establishments and been recognised as being applicable to a wide range of situations.

In its most basic form, morphological analysis is nothing more than generating ideas by means of a matrix. So, for example, a matrix of two axes, with ten items on each axis, produces $10 \times 10 = 100$ combinations of items, or ideas. Make the matrix a three-dimensional cube, by adding another axis of ten items, and $100 \times 10 = 1000$ combinations or ideas are produced. Add yet another dimension and the multiplying effect continues (this is impossible to draw, but possible to imagine, as 1000 elements are combined with each of 10 items on a 'fourth-dimensional' axis to yield 10,000 ideas).

Here are some examples of different levels of morphological analysis.

Two-dimensional matrix
A firm manufacturing umbrellas wants to extend its range into more specialised and unusual products. The company is searching for new ideas.

The first stage is to identify suitable categories of ideas to use as the axes of a matrix, bearing in mind that one is seeking to discover opportunities rather than come up with an immediate solution. In this case, the axes could be 'utilities' (the extra features customers might value which could be built into an umbrella) and 'venue' (places or situations in which the umbrella might be used). If these axes were chosen, the matrix might look like this:

UTILITIES

VENUE	Flask	Calculator	Radio	Anti-mugging alarm	Alarm clock/stop-watch	Compass	Telescope	Battery-operated fan	Camera	Tool kit	Storage compartment
Journeys to work											
Golf courses											
Cricket matches											
School sports											
Walking holidays											
Horse races											
Air shows											
Gardens or parks											
Tennis matches											
Cities											
Beach holidays											

Figure 22   An example of a two dimensional matrix

This example shows a matrix of 11 × 11 = 121 items, and it is clearly possible to add many more items to each axis. From such a reservoir of ideas, the odds of finding one or two good ones must be greatly increased.

Three-dimensional matrix

A container manufacturer wants to come up with some new packaging ideas which will enable it to develop new markets.

Again the key to success is to find suitable axes which are pertinent to the problem. For example, the three-dimensional matrix might look something like this:

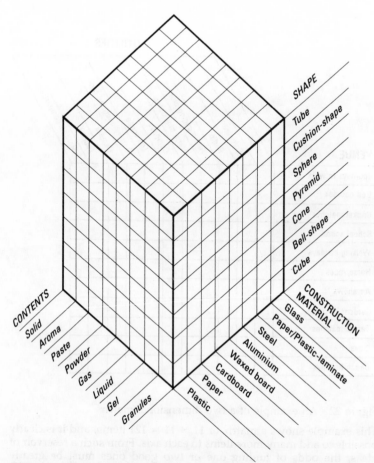

Figure 23 An example of a three-dimensional matrix

Adapted from Simon Majaro, *International Marketing – A Strategic Approach to World Markets* (London: George Allen & Unwin, 1986).

With these axes – contents, material and shape – 8 × 8 × 7 = 448 combinations or ideas are generated. Moveover, in this example, just one addition to the shape axis would yield another 64 ideas. Even from the original 448 ideas, it should be statistically possible to expect some seven or eight potential winners.

Four-dimensional matrix

A manufacturer in the disposable containers business wants to develop some new products.

As we have already noted, it is impossible to represent four-dimensional morphological analysis visually. This is a shame because diagrams and pictures can often stimulate the imagination much more effectively than words alone. Nevertheless, in its relentless and somewhat mechanical way, this technique is probably unsurpassed in terms of generating ideas.

As with all types of morphological analysis, the success of this approach depends on the ability to choose pertinent dimensions. Here are some possible axis headings and items.

	Material	Shape	Content	Venue
1	Paper	Balloon	Coffee	Rambling
2	Polystyrene	Beaker	Fruit Juice	Cycling
3				
4				
5				
6				
7				
8				
9				
10				

Above, or on a separate piece of paper, attempt to expand each of the columns to ten items – in other words generate 10,000 ideas.

Evaluating the ideas

With its enormous potential for generating ideas, morphological analysis poses something of a problem for those faced with evaluating the results. Clearly, to be confronted with a computer print-out of 10,000 combinations or ideas is a daunting prospect. Fortunately there are two methods which help to simplify the task.

Ideas in clusters

Instead of focusing on each idea in turn, the ideas can be considered in clusters, for example, the 'paper–balloon–coffee' combination could be assessed against each 'venue' entry. This helps trim the original list to manageable proportions. Moreover, evaluating clusters of ideas against the items in one column tends to focus attention on that column, and often new entries emerge at the evaluation session, for example: 'Could this combination be used in the military services?' 'on aircraft?' and so on.

Multi-phase screening

This works on the principle that creative people often find it easier to screen ideas displayed in visual form. This can still be achieved for a four-dimensional matrix if the first three axes are displayed as a cube. The best ideas are selected from this and then examined in combination with the fourth axis by using a two-dimensional matrix. If there happened to be a fifth axis as well, a new cube could be constructed using the best of the screened ideas from the first cube in combination with the two remaining axes.

Facilities

The ideal facilities for a morphological analysis session are similar to those for other idea-generating techniques: a quiet, suitably-sized room equipped with flip-chart or wall board, pens and comfortable chairs. Seating should be arranged to allow for maximum interaction between group members, thus a circular formation is preferable. It is useful to have some blank two- and three-dimensional matrices on hand, for example, some $6 \times 6 \times 6$ cubes for warm-ups and $12 \times 12 \times 12$ cubes for the main task.

Number of participants

A group of about 6–8 people seems to work quite well.

Roles

There is one key role, that of leader. This person needs to be:

- familiar with the subject
- capable of communicating enthusiastically
- able to keep a steady momentum going in the group. Once started, breaks in the process can reduce the level of creativity, rather as if the 'magic' wears off.

There is no need for a scribe, as in brainstorming, because group members record their own data, which is later collated by the leader.

Experience suggests that a morphological analysis group does not perform so well if

User's comments

'inexperienced' guest members occasionally participate.

Procedure

Step 1 *Explain the technique.* It is important that everyone understands the method to be used. The main problems that groups experience seem to centre on the selection of the dimensions which relate to the problem under review. Identifying these dimensions is often the result of more 'analytical' (as opposed to 'creative') thought processes. It will be valuable to remind the group members that:

- The chosen dimensions must be relevant to the problem and have some logical inter-relationship, so, for example, in the search for a new perfume it would be legitimate to consider fragrance (spicy, musky, citron, etc.), container shape and target market, among other dimensions.
- While the dimensions themselves need to be appropriate and interrelated, the items listed under each dimension can be as off-beat as one chooses (perhaps the result of brainstorming). For example, on the fragrance axis mentioned above, it would be valid to list the smells of frying bacon, sea breezes, newly cut grass and so on.

Step 2 *Warm-up.* As with most creative-thinking sessions, some mental limbering up will lead to a more productive meeting. It is particularly useful to focus the warm-up on the selection of dimensions for morphological analysis. This can be done by giving all participants some blank cubes like the ones overleaf.

Ask the group to identify appropriate matrix dimensions for test cases such as the following:

- a bank seeking to identify new products or services for its customers (e.g. type of customer, venue of service, type of service, etc.)

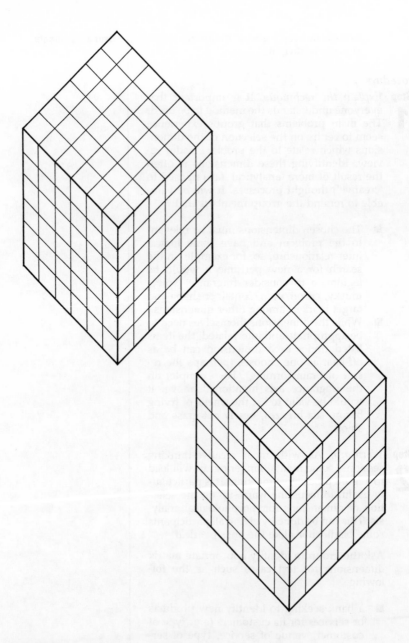

Figure 24   a blank three-dimensional matrix cubes for a warm up session.

- a football club attempting to increase its attendance figures (e.g. additional facilities/entertainment, type of publicity, type of customer, etc.)
- a food company wishing to invent a new dish (e.g. type of food, method of cooking, presentation/packaging, etc.)
- an inventor develops a new type of vehicle to compete with the motor car (e.g. shape, means of propulsion, materials, etc.)
- a telephone company looking for new ideas for an additional telephone service (e.g. type of customer, type of service, compatability with other kinds of equipment, etc.)

Allow discussion about the dimensions that participants choose, because it is necessary for the group as a whole to agree on them before proceeding to list items. Often two dimensions can be agreed quite quickly, it is the third one which can prove controversial.

After about 30 minutes stop the warm-up session and review it to check what lessons have been learned which could be carried over into the main session. If participants are having difficulty identifying or agreeing about dimensions, continue with another warm-up exercise.

Step *Defining the task.* Before starting the morphological analysis on the task in hand, it is important to clarify and define the issue into a simple, unambiguous statement, for example, 'to identify new applications for worn car tyres'. This concise statement should be written on the flip-chart or wall board to act as a reminder during the creative process.

Step 4 *The task itself.* First the group must agree on the various dimensions of the matrix. Initially participants should work on the task individually, then share their dimensions with the group. If more than three suitable dimensions are identified, the group should try to determine their relative importance and priority. In many ways three-dimensional matrices are easiest for new groups to handle, and are certainly visually stimulating. Sometimes the group might experiment by constructing cubes|with various different third dimensions.

Once the dimensions have been agreed, the group can list items for each one, using whatever free-wheeling, idea-generating processes it prefers. When ideas for items are no longer forthcoming, it is time to bring the session to a halt.

The task then facing the group is to identify the best prospects from the great number of ideas generated. This can be achieved by using one or several of the following methods:

- listing the five most exciting ideas among the myriad cells of the matrix
- identifying the five most absurd ideas and then using them as 'intermediate impossibles' to lead to workable ones
- picking up a few of the most worthwhile-looking ideas and attempting to visualise how they will work in practice over the next few years. The scenario day-dreaming technique discussed later in the section could be useful at this stage.
- using a screening matrix which identifies the 'excellent/excellent' ideas (see Section 6).

Suitable topics for morphological analysis

Since this technique is ideal for generating a large number of ideas of an explorary or opportunity-seeking nature, it is particularly useful to apply to problems whose solutions are likely to be creative or unexpected combinations of two or more elements, for example:

- new product or service variants
- applications for new materials
- new market segments and/or applications

- new ways of developing a competitive advantage
- novel promotional techniques for products or services
- identification of new location opportunities.

Unsuitable topics for morphological analysis

This technique is not likely to be very helpful:

- where there can only be one solution or where the group has to focus on a narrow band of options
- where the remit is very limited
- for any situation or problem which is known to have only one dimension, for example, finding an alternative packaging for a specific tomato ketchup.

User's comments

Scenario writing and scenario day-dreaming

Anyone who has ever been involved in business planning will be aware that it is not just a simple matter of extrapolating past data into the future. Like a motorist driving along a highway, the planner certainly needs to check in the rear-view mirror from time to time, but should primarily be concerned with looking ahead, where the major obstacles, dangers and opportunities lie.

Unfortunately many companies tend to take a rear-view mirror approach to planning because looking ahead is too difficult. Of course the future can never be predicted with perfect accuracy. Yet organisations which manage to anticipate future events are in a much stronger position to devise strategies and allocate resources to cope with them successfully.

Scenario writing and scenario day-dreaming are two versions of a predictive technique which enables an organisation to remove some of the uncertainty from the future, and to be better prepared for it when it arrives.

Scenario writing

This technique was developed as an approach to long-term planning and technological forecasting. One of the pioneers in this field, Herman Kahn, suggested that the main benefits arising from scenario writing are that it forces a planning team:

- to reduce the 'carry-over' thinking of the past
- to 'plunge into the unfamiliar and rapidly changing world of the present and future by dramatising and illustrating the possibilities they focus on'
- to tackle details and dynamics which they might easily neglect if they restricted themselves to abstract considerations (Kahn and Weiner, 1967).

Being forced to consider the future in a deliberate and systematic way tends to make an organisation's management more receptive to both change and the need for creative thinking. Ultimately, the most valuable aspect of scenario writing is not its accuracy, but the fact that managers have shared a process which has opened their minds to new possibilities and opportunities. In this way, it is instrumental in enriching corporate creativity and opening the door to innovation. This point is completely missed by companies who take the easy way out by engaging outside consultants to prepare their future scenarios. Although the final document might look more professional than an internally produced one, managers will never have the same level of commitment to it, as they would have to the product of their own collective creative efforts.

Facilities

For the briefing and scenario-sharing sessions (Steps 1 and 3) facilities are similar to those for other idea-generating techniques. A quiet, suitably-sized room should provide a relaxed environment and be equipped with the necessary visual aids and writing materials.

Roles

A leader/facilitator is needed to chair the briefing session and the final discussion and to co-ordinate the preparation of the final document.

Each scenario-writer must be an 'expert' in his or her given field. Since expertise is a more important consideration for group membership than seniority, there might be occasions when a participant is not a senior manager. This is often the case in research or design work. Unless the organisation is extremely hierarchical and status-conscious, the inclusion of a non-manager should not present an insurmountable problem. The types of experts invited to participate will naturally be tailored to the nature of the organisation's activities and concerns, thus a manufacturer

User's comments

of baby products might assemble a team whose areas of expertise included demographics, child-psychology, social analysis and paediatrics, as well as market analysts in this area, production managers and so on.

Procedure

Step *Briefing.* Members of the group are asked to anticipate developments in their areas of specialisation over the next five or ten years and to assess the impact, favourable or otherwise, of these future events and trends on the company. Each participant is asked to support his or her predictions with evidence, which can come from reports from national or international forecasting bodies, speeches by authorative figures, and so on.

Step *Individual scenario writing.* After the briefing session, each manager goes away to prepare his or her particular scenario independently, producing a short written paper for later presentation to the group. In order to maintain momentum and interest in the project, not too much time should be allowed for this stage, say two weeks.

Step *Collective scenario writing.* The group meets again and the individual papers are presented and discussed until a consensus view can be agreed. This is then set out in a formal written document (produced by the leader and/or a small committee of participants) which is submitted as input to the company's strategic thinking.

Strengths of scenario writing

Scenario writing is a particularly useful exercise when a large number of factors affect the firm and its business environment. It enables planners to highlight the most significant areas of change and devise future strategies accordingly. Situations where scenario writing has been used with a high level of success include:

- the food and beverage industry, where certain forward-looking companies identified the move towards healthier lifestyles much earlier than others
- the air transport industry, where trends for more exotic holiday locations and increased personal air travel, as opposed to business travel, were identified
- personnel planning, where an organisation needs to foresee what types of people and skills it will require in order to remain successful in the future.

Weaknesses of scenario writing

While there is much to commend this technique, there are also some drawbacks:

- Because it is a complex, challenging and time-consuming project, scenario writing is not undertaken very frequently. As a result, people within the organisation tend to view the few scenario documents which are produced as lacking credibility or value.
- The fact that the company 'experts' involved are often senior managers makes scenario writing appear to be an elitist exercise. This greatly reduces the potential of the project to stimulate creative change within the organisation. Care must be taken to prevent the alienation or indifference of middle and operational management, by involving as many levels of the organisation as possible in the preliminary stages and interpretation of the scenario-writing project.
- Completely unpredictable, far-reaching events may take place which render the written scenario obsolete. However, in such circumstances, plans based on past performance are equally irrelevant. At least scenario writing can encourage managers to be future-orientated, which may enable them to respond more effectively to unforeseen developments.

User's comments

Scenario day-dreaming

Scenario day-dreaming is similar to scenario writing in that its aim is to formulate a comprehensive, plausible vision of the future and its implications for the organisation. Scenario day-dreaming is a less formal exercise, however, in which no written report is produced. The entire process takes place verbally, often during a two-day session. Participants are not asked to research and produce individual reports nor (necessarily) to substantiate their views with evidence. As a result, the output of scenario day-dreaming might be less valid for planning purposes, but what the technique lacks in analysis and supporting data, it makes up for in its ability to stimulate people's imaginations and encourage them to think on broader horizons and explore their more unusual or unprovable ideas.

Facilities

Scenario day-dreaming should take place over a period of two days or so, at a venue which allows participants to concentrate fully on the exercise. For this reason the session should be held away from the organisation's premises, at a hotel, an academic institution during vacation, a conference centre, or the like. Amenities should be comfortable but not overly luxurious, or they may distract from the task in hand. Participants should agree to devote their complete attention to the proceedings, which entails avoiding use of the telephone or contacting their offices at any time during the session.

The main meeting room should be comfortable and well-lit, and equipped with a round table, overhead projector, flip-charts, writing pads and coloured pens. Since the group may be split into small groups or syndicates for certain exercises, two or three smaller rooms should be available nearby. (Sometimes alcoves or quiet corners off the main room are sufficient for this.)

Number of participants

Eight to ten people plus a leader seems to be a good number. With a group of this size, the plenary group is still not too large but there is scope for two or three syndicates.

User's comments

111

Roles

Leader. In great part the success of scenario day-dreaming depends on having an experienced leader. If there is no such person within the organisation, an outside facilitator should be engaged. The leader's role involves:

- planning the session in detail
- advising on the selection of participants
- briefing participants about what is expected of them, both in terms of the topics to be considered and the 'rules' for successful idea-generation
- leading the session
- motivating and stimulating the group, which includes judging when the participants might benefit from a switch to a different type of idea-generating technique
- helping to summarise the conclusions and useful ideas which emerge from the session.

Participants. The team members invited to take part in the scenario day-dreaming session should be men and women who:
- generally exhibit some of the characteristics of creative individuals outlined in Section 4
- are capable of looking at the organisation's activities in a broad, objective and imaginative way
- do not have egocentric or parochial attitudes
- are tolerant of both new ideas and ambiguity
- have specific expertise in areas which will have significant impact on the future of the organisation's activities
- have experience of working across functional boundaries in the organisation, in other words, have some feel for what others are doing.

Ideally one or two members of top management should be included in order to impart status and legitimacy to the team (even so, these people should also meet the other criteria).

It is not necessary to have a scribe, but a member of the group should keep minutes of the proceedings (this task may be rotated among participants) and note the ideas which emerge during the course of the exercise. Otherwise potentially valuable and innovative ideas may be lost.

Procedure

Step *Preparation.* The leader sends out a briefing document in advance, to inform participants of the objectives of the session and give details of how it will be run. This document should stress the importance of participants remaining positive and open-minded throughout the exercise. (This should ensure that the leader does not have occasion to criticise group members in front of their colleagues during the session itself.) The briefing paper should also emphasise that participants are requested to arrange not to be contacted by work colleagues during the session. Finally, it should explain that group members who wish to bring along supporting evidence for their specialised contributions are free to do so.

Step 2 *The scenario day-dreaming session.* Since scenario day-dreaming takes place over two days, it is divided into a number of shorter sessions which give the exercise a structure of beginning, middle and end. Without a carefully controlled overall structure, much of the momentum and usefulness of the technique will be lost.

Day one

Introduction and warm-up

The participants are introduced to each other (if they have not met before) and invited to say a few words about themselves. The leader explains how the session is going to be run, reviews the day-dreaming technique and answers any questions that members of the group may have about the exercise.

The leader conducts a warm-up session to relax the group and illustrate the day-dreaming technique. Useful topics for warm-up sessions include:

- 'Consider a scenario for tourism in the year 2000.'
- 'Consider a scenario for education in the year 2000.'
- 'Consider a scenario for health in the year 2000.'

Obviously the participants are unlikely to be experts in these fields, but at the same time they will have been tourists, patients, students or parents at some time or other and will certainly have a wide range of views. During this exercise the leader should encourage the group to think about changes in social conditions, attitudes, politics, the economy, the environment and the infrastructure that may take place by the year 2000 and thus influence their scenario.

After about half an hour the group should have developed a scenario for its warm-up topic. This should then be reviewed, and any issues that helped or hindered the groups functioning should be discussed so that the team can work even more effectively on its main task.

At this point, the leader decides whether the team is ready to proceed or whether another warm-up exercise is necessary. If a second warm-up is chosen, a shorter length of time, say about 20 minutes, should be allowed for it.

Identifying the main factors

The purpose of this very important step in the proceedings is to determine the various factors which are likely to impinge on the future success of the organisation. These factors will become the basis of the scenario day-dreaming exercise proper, and will naturally vary from company to company. The following list (although by no means comprehensive) may be used to stimulate discussion of possible factors to be explored. The leader

User's comments

may wish to draw up his or her own set of suggestions or to initiate a brief brainstorming session in which participants generate a number of further ideas.

Trigger list of factors to be explored during a scenario day-dreaming session

Factor for exploration	Possible issues in future
Economic trends	■ Inflation ■ Purchasing power of customer groups ■ Government spending ■ Fiscal policy ■ Exchange rates ■ Expenditure on the infra-structure
Cost of commodities and raw materials	■ Impact on production costs ■ Substitute materials ■ Market pressure for new materials ■ Availability of scarce materials ■ Cartels or political blocs
National and international politics (including changes in traditional alliances, possible geopolitical unrest)	■ Disappearing traditional markets ■ Emergence of new markets ■ New competition ■ New 'rules' for conducting business
Military developments and general security issues	■ Impact on R & D ■ Impact on arms and allied industries

	■ Government spending ■ Demand for engineers, new technology ■ New applications for defence technology
Paramilitary developments (including the need to combat terrorism)	■ Safer travel v. increased costs ■ Personal liberties v. spot checks ■ Better personal security systems ■ Better communication systems ■ Community action
Demographics	■ Changes in birth-rate ■ Life expectancy ■ Market segment factors
Changes in legal and quasi-legal regulations	■ Safety ■ Tariffs and quotas ■ Employment legislation ■ EEC regulations
Consumer life-style	■ Work ■ Leisure ■ Disposable income ■ Homes ■ Shopping ■ Hobbies
Technological changes	■ Impact on production ■ Facilities required

		User's comments
	■ Skills and staffing ■ Costs v. benefits ■ Uses for old technology	
Institutional developments	■ Channels of distribution ■ Media and communications ■ Retailing practices ■ Banking and finance arrangements ■ Education	
Social structure	■ Distribution of wealth ■ Social welfare systems ■ Level of employment ■ Social pressures ■ Lobby groups	
Ecology and the environment	■ Banned materials or processes ■ Approved procedures ■ Pollution and its control ■ Standards and costs ■ Location ■ Legislation ■ Pressure groups ■ Transport ■ Product design and obsolescence	
Information technology	■ Office automation ■ Data processing	

	■ Transfer of funds ■ New applications ■ Stock control and reordering ■ New expertise required
Infrastructural developments (e.g. Channel tunnel, new motorways or airports, closure of railway lines)	■ Effects on logistics ■ Impact on labour market ■ New markets ■ New competition ■ Applications for new products or services
Changes in consumer attitudes	■ Packaging ■ Additives and colourings ■ Health issues ■ Value
Changes in consumer habits	■ Sport and leisure ■ Outdoor activities ■ Sex and marriage ■ Holidays ■ Spending patterns
Biotechnology	■ Developments ■ New applications ■ Facilities
Consumers' attitudes towards savings and capital accumulation	■ Share owning ■ Home owning ■ Mortgage rates ■ Fiscal policy/tax levels ■ New services ■ Banks and financial institutions

There are two major aims at this stage of the proceedings:

■ to identify and assign priorities to the most important factors for consideration, relative to the organisation's activities and needs
■ to create an atmosphere in which the group is so engrossed in its imagined future world that participants feel that they are actually seeing and analysing their organisation's role in its future environment.

Of course it is more difficult to achieve this second objective, but the payoff from this kind of collective imaginative leap – in terms of creativity, morale and *esprit de corps* – is considerable. It is well worth engaging an experienced professional facilitator who can maintain the momentum necessary to reach this sustained level of future-orientation in the group.

After the main factors for consideration have been discussed and agreed, they should be summarised on a flip-chart in order of priority.

Scenario day-dreaming
At this point the group moves on to scenario day-dreaming proper. This stage of the proceedings will probably take place over the afternoon sessions of the first day and the morning sessions of the second day. For this activity the group is split into smaller groups or syndicates of no fewer than three participants.

Each syndicate is assigned several of the important factors identified by the group in the previous activity; the syndicates' task is to consider each individual factor in depth and arrive at a future scenario for each one. The leader should take care over both the composition of the syndicates and the topics assigned to each one, to ensure that participants' abilities and expertise are logically combined and well matched to the factors to be considered. For example, it would be fruitless to assign the topic 'changing technology' to a group whose members possessed no knowledge of this field. After the syndicates have been operating for a time, the leader might decide to reshuffle the groupings to provide fresh stimulus to the proceedings.

Syndicates should be allowed about 30 minutes to produce a scenario for each factor. For each scenario, a member of the syndicate takes the necessary notes to make a presentation later to the plenary group. It is good practice for syndicate members to perform this task in rotation so that participants present at least one scenario apiece.

Day two
Presentation and discussion of syndicates' scenarios

Scenario day-dreaming in syndicates continues during the morning sessions until all of the factors for consideration have been dealt with. The entire group then reassembles in plenary session to hear the syndicates' presentations of individual scenarios.

The plenary group discusses each scenario in order to reach consensus about the various hypotheses submitted and to identify and eliminate contradictions with scenarios offered by other syndicates. When all the scenarios have been heard and analysed, the group is ready for the very important task of integrating them into a single, comprehensive vision of the future. The leader's role in this undertaking is to guide the group towards unanimity.

Idea generation in response to the scenario

The plenary group divides into syndicates again in order to consider the agreed future scenario and submit ideas as to how the organisation can respond to the opportunities and threats it involves. At this stage the

User's comments

syndicates may use any creative-thinking techniques (brainstorming, metaphorical analogy, morphological analysis, etc.) which they feel would be useful, keeping a record of the ideas which emerge.

Closing session
The plenary group then reconvenes to discuss and explore the syndicates' ideas. At the end of the session, the leader reviews the proceedings and summarises the group's perception of things to come and its suggestions as to how the organisation can best meet the challenges of the future.

At the discretion of the sponsoring organisation, the leader may or may not be asked to produce a short 'vision' document summarising the group's conclusion. On the one hand, some organisations might feel that valuable ideas which emerged from the session would be lost unless they were recorded in a report. On the other hand, some organisations might feel that the true value of the exercise lies in the process of scenario day-dreaming itself, and in its enriching impact on participants, so that a written record is unnecessary. In cases of doubt, the leader may advise the organisation whether or not a report would be useful.

User's comments

Suitable topics for scenario day - dreaming

It should be quite clear by now that this technique is particularly helpful in situations which demand a longer-term perspective. It is especially appropriate in disengaging an organisation's strategic or middle managers from day-to-day issues and projecting them into a future environment with all its potential to stimulate creative ideas for development. Some examples of suitable projects for scenario day-dreaming are included in the following list:

- defining the firm's mission statement
- searching for strategies to maintain or improve market position
- developing a competitive advantage in the future
- identifying companies to acquire or merge with
- developing new products or markets
- identifying locations and/or countries where the company's products could be manufactured more productively in the future
- identifying ways to develop tomorrow's managers.

Trigger session

Most creative idea-generating techniques work on the assumption that people are most forthcoming with ideas in a relaxed, non-threatening environment. However, with some people or in certain companies, a slightly competitive atmosphere is needed to get the adrenalin flowing. Trigger sessions capitalise on the 'healthy competition' aspect of working together. Unlike brainstorming, this technique puts participants under some emotional pressure to generate good ideas.

The facilities, number of participants and leader's role in trigger sessions are generally similar to those for other creativity techniques, such as brainstorming.

Procedure	User's comments

Step *Independent idea-generation.* The group is presented with a problem to solve. Each member is given a blank sheet of paper and invited to write down as many ideas for solving the problem as possible. Participants work silently and independently; there is no interaction as in brainstorming. Approximately 10 minutes is allowed for this stage.

Step *Discussion and group idea-generation.* Each member reads his or her ideas to the group and they are recorded on a flip-chart or overhead projector. The group then considers these 'trigger' ideas, looking for ways of embellishing them or combining them into further ideas. Each new variation is recorded until a large and diverse quantity of ideas has been produced.

Step *Evaluation.* The ideas are then evaluated and the most promising ones selected for possible implementation.

Suitable and unsuitable topics for trigger sessions are similar to those described for brainstorming sessions.

Wildest idea session

This is a systematic attempt at generating outrageous ideas, which are subsequently examined for possible realistic applications to the problem under consideration. This technique represents a way of overcoming the self-censorship which prevents many people from expressing their most 'preposterous' ideas, which are often the ones richest in creative potential.

The facilities, group size and leader's role are similar to those for the other 'short session' idea-generating techniques examined in this section.

Procedure
Suppose a company wants to reduce its annual bill for photocopying.

Step 1 *Idea-generation.* Rather like in brainstorming, the problem–solving group is encouraged to call out ideas which could alleviate this problem, but with the clearly-understood proviso that the ideas must be as outrageous as possible. The ideas are recorded on a flip-chart. They might include:

- Don't repair the photocopier when it breaks down.
- Move it and don't tell anybody its new location.
- It only can be used in lunchbreaks or after work.
- Don't reorder any copying paper.
- Arrange for it to break down for 10 minutes after every 3 copies.
- It explodes when people use it.
- The machine is rigged to give users electric shocks of increasing severity as they make more copies.
- A photograph is taken of the user and the number of copies made is logged.
- Set the machine to run off 1000 copies each time.
- Make it coin-operated to take only Nepalese currency.

Step 2 *Discussion and evaluation.* The group now returns to reality and evaluates the list of ideas. The point of the exercise is to choose the wildest idea and salvage some usable elements from it. In this way the wildest ideas become stepping-stones, or 'intermediate impossibles', to practical, creative solutions. Thus, the group might conclude that while it might not be feasible to blow people up or electrocute them without incurring the wrath of HM Factory Inspectorate, it might be possible to impose some kind of penalty for excessive use of the photocopier.

In fact the company in this example limited the hours in which the copier was operative and issued all users with what was considered to be a reasonable allocation of copying paper. Anyone who ran over this amount had to sign a book to explain why, before more

User's comments

124

paper was issued. A monthly prize was awarded to the person who used least copying paper.

The wildest idea technique is certainly great fun to use. It can shake even the most inhibited group member out of a rigid frame of mind because it encourages people to think broadly and eccentrically. For this reason it can be a very useful technique to use as a warm-up exercise or to help a flagging group regain its creative impetus.

A variation on the wildest idea technique is to combine it with a trigger session in the following way.

Step *Idea generation.* The problem-solving group is given paper and, as in a trigger session, asked to write down as many outrageous ideas as possible for solving the problem.

Step *Circulation and embellishment of ideas.* After about 5 minutes each person passes his or her list to the person on the left (or right – the direction is immaterial so long as consistency is maintained and lists never return to their orginators). Participants then build on the ideas in the lists they have been passed, using them to generate even more outrageous ideas. They add their new ideas to the list.

This process is repeated several more times.

Step 3 *Development of ideas.* The lists are passed to the left once more, and one by one participants read aloud the one or two most outrageous ideas on the lists in front of them. No one is promoting his or her own ideas at this stage, because everyone is reading from a new list.

The ideas are recorded on a flip-chart as they are read out. The group attempts to develop some usable ideas from this list and these are noted for possible future action.

Suitable and unsuitable topics for wildest idea sessions are similar to those described for brainstorming sessions.

Suggestion schemes

A properly run suggestion scheme represents a valuable method for tapping the vast reservoir of ideas locked away in the minds of an organisation's staff, visitors, clients or customers. It is a regrettable fact, however, that many suggestion schemes fail to generate much enthusiasm or response from their target audiences. Such poor responses almost invariably indicate that schemes have not been adequately planned or managed, because successful schemes require much more effort than merely scattering suggestion boxes around an organisation's premises.

To be effective, a suggestion scheme must be planned in detail, carefully implemented and intelligently managed. There are a number of factors which must be skilfully developed and co-ordinated to ensure the success of a suggestion scheme, but two of the most important conditions are:

- The suggestion scheme must receive the full commitment and participation of top management.
- A suggestion scheme has a much greater chance of success if it is part of a deliberate, full-scale, well-integrated programme to promote creativity and innovation within the organisation.

The following guidelines will help an organisation set up a workable suggestion scheme capable of inspiring submissions and sustaining the confidence and good will of its target audience.

Step 1 *Set clear objectives for the scheme.* A suggestion scheme should be designed in response to clearly defined objectives. The primary general objective will usually be to invite ideas from the organisation's staff or custom-

User's comments

ers, but a firm might wish to focus this objective more narrowly by requesting submissions on specific areas of concern, for example, increasing sales, improving customer relations, or reducing down time.

Organisations should be aware that there may also be a number of secondary objectives which a suggestion scheme can be designed to address, for example:

■ to emphasise the firm's commitment to creativity and innovation
■ to improve customer relations by showing that the firm cares about its clients' preferences and opinions
■ to improve personnel relations by showing that the firm values and encourages the creative potential of its employees
■ to break down barriers between senior management and other levels in the organisation.

After the objectives of the suggestion scheme have been decided, both the management of the scheme and the general climate of the organisation must genuinely and actively reflect the desire to achieve them. Of course, one of the objectives might be to improve the organisation's climate, and again it must be emphasised that without the consistent and unequivocal support of management, starting from the top levels, any efforts in this direction will justifiably be dismissed as corporate window-dressing. Any undertaking, such as a suggestion scheme, which operates on a voluntary principle is a good litmus test of staff attitudes towards an organisation. If employees are suspicious and disaffected, they will simply fail to come forward with ideas, and in such a case, honest efforts must be made to remedy the causes of dissatisfaction before a suggestion scheme can be expected to work.

Step 2 *Work out the details of the scheme.* There are three main issues regarding the operation of any suggestion scheme which must be settled in advance:

- How should ideas be submitted?
- How should ideas be assessed?
- What rewards should be offered to the submitters of winning ideas?

Submitting ideas.
Procedures for submitting suggestions should be as user-friendly as possible to encourage as wide a cross-section of the workforce as possible (including managers) to volunteer ideas. There should be a sufficient number of centrally-placed collection points such as suggestion boxes or the like.

Some organisations may decide that a standardised format for submissions is desirable in order to facilitate screening and feedback procedures or emphasise particular objectives of the suggestion scheme. For example, if the organisation's major objective is seeking ideas for reducing costs, a standard form could be designed to include a space where the cost-saving merits of ideas could be explained. If a standard form is used, it too should be as user-friendly and non-bureaucratic as possible, and employees should not be penalised for volunteering their ideas in a different format.

Assessing ideas

Any consideration of assessment methods must address the questions of who makes up the screening panel, what evaluation procedures are used, and how assessments are communicated back to submitters.

The members of an organisation's evaluation panel must be fully in sympathy both with the objectives of the suggestion scheme and with the attempt to involve the organisation as a whole in the creativity and innovation process. Panel members should be creative people themselves (on the principle that it takes creative people to recognise creative ideas), and should be known to be impartial and receptive to the ideas of others. The team should represent a wide range of skills and experience and include participants from all levels of the organisation. Volunteers who meet these requirements should be preferred to members who must be asked to participate, since the former are obviously highly motivated and sympathetic to the aims of the scheme. Finally the membership of the assessment panel should be rotated occasionally both in order to involve a wider range of people (this increases awareness and support for the suggestion scheme throughout the organisation) and to maintain freshness of mind and enthusiasm among panel members.

Having clear, definite procedures for screening ideas is preferable to merely discussing them on an *ad hoc* basis. Assessing suggestions against an agreed set of criteria ensures that:

- ideas receive fairer and more rigorous analysis
- the evaluation panel does not become overwhelmed and confused by a welter of different ideas
- the credibility of the panel (and of the suggestion scheme itself) is enhanced and people remain willing to volunteer ideas because they believe the evaluation process is serious, fair and careful.

A number of methods for screening ideas is discussed in Section 6.

Ideas should be screened regularly (e.g. every month or every few months) and the results promptly communicated back to the individuals who submitted them. Acknowledging and responding to suggestions punctually is one of the most important means of ensuring that volunteers continue to submit them. It reassures participants that the suggestion scheme is taken seriously and managed competently, and it also cuts down on unnecessary expense. The evaluation panel should take care that negative responses to ideas do not appear to be harsh or unimaginative, or involve rejec-

User's comments

tion of the individuals who submitted them. After thanking the volunteer for the suggestion, a brief, clear explanation of why the idea is not possible to implement is sufficient. Responses which imply that the organisation maintains a rigid, negative attitude to the new ideas (e.g. 'Your ideas is incompatible with company policy.') should be avoided.

Rewarding ideas
Financial prizes (although they may play some part in a reward system) are often not the most motivating or satisfying awards for winning submissions. Well-publicised acknowledgement of good ideas and of their value to the organisation, and information about how they will be implemented are frequently most gratifying to the individuals who submitted them and most inspiring to other contributors who aspire to similar recognition.

An organisation's appreciation for winning ideas may be formalised by a regular 'creativity' section in the company newsletter or magazine or by a permanent creativity roll of honour. Measures such as these demonstrate an enduring commitment to the promotion and recognition of creativity and innovation and help to entrench this commitment in the corporate culture.

Other possible rewards include:

- vouchers or prizes such as theatre tickets, holiday breaks, etc.
- certificates of merit presented by senior executives
- taking employees' creative efforts into consideration during salary and promotion reviews.

Step 3 *Promote the scheme.* Adequate publicity is vital to the success of a suggestion scheme. In fact, the scheme should be as professionally 'marketed' to its target audience as the organisation's products are to its target market – and indeed, it may be appropriate to involve the marketing department in its promotion. The organisers must make certain that the aims of the scheme, its submissions and screening procedures, intervals of assessment and response, and types of reward are thoroughly publicised.

Sufficient promotion guarantees that:

■ everyone who may have suggestions knows how to submit them
■ people's expectations of the scheme are realistic
■ the target audience understands the organisation's commitment to the project.

In addition, communicating the scheme's objectives and methods of evaluation can encourage a certain amount of self-screening, in which volunteers submit only those ideas which they feel are relevant and have a good chance of impressing the assessment panel. This results in better suggestions and reduces the work-load of the evaluations.

Step 4 *Communicating results.* Communicating results forms part of the overall promotion of the suggestion scheme and helps to maintain interest, commitment and the flow of ideas. For each period of, say, six months or a year, the following details should be publicised:

■ a list of the number and types of suggestions received
■ brief descriptions of the five or so best ideas, how they were implemented and why they were particularly valuable to the organisation
■ an analysis of how well the specific objectives of the suggestion scheme are being met
■ information about the individuals who submitted winning ideas and about the rewards they received.

This information may be conveyed through the in-house newsletter and various other promotional methods, for example, a version of the 'creatometer' mentioned in Section 3, which – rather like the devices used in charity appeals – shows how well the level and quality of ideas approach a certain target.

Step 5 *Monitor and review the scheme.* It is good practice for the organisers of a suggestion scheme to conduct a yearly assessment of its results, canvassing and inviting recommendations for improvement from various levels of the organisation: management, the assessment panel, volunteers of ideas and any other relevant groups or individuals. This yearly assessment is a good opportunity to give the scheme a new lease of life. The suggestions it elicits should be carefully considered, implemented if appropriate, and the improvements communicated to the organisation as a whole. The more stakeholders a suggestion scheme has, the greater its chances of continued success.

As an alternative to a full-scale suggestion scheme, an organisation can sponsor one-off competitions for winning ideas on specific topics, such as 'How can the company attract a satisfactory number of talented trainees in the next few years, when there will be increasing competition for well-qualified young recruits?' Like full-scale suggestion schemes, such *ad hoc* competitions should involve rigorous screening procedures and appropriate publicity and rewards.

User's comments

Think Tanks

Think Tanks were introduced in Section 4 on pages 69–70. In order to ensure that such groups are cost-effective in terms of creativity and innovation, sponsoring organisations should see to it that they are structured, managed, led and stimulated as positively and systematically as possible.

As we saw in Section 4, Think Tanks must have clearly defined, specific objectives. Any deadlines related to such objectives must be clearly understood by everyone involved, and progress rigorously monitored without creating an unproductive atmosphere of pressure or panic. It is important, especially at the beginning of a Think Tank's activities, to 'build in' a certain degree of success by including some readily achievable goals among its objectives. The group's first tangible results should relate to tasks which – without being trivial – are relatively easy to accomplish and are of genuine, obvious benefit to the organisation. A few strategic early successes are good both for morale within the Think Tank and for the group's 'public relations' within the larger organisation.

Unless the aims and contributions of the Think Tank are confidential, they should be communicated within the organisation. Every effort should be made to ensure that the group is perceived as a valued, active and well-integrated part of the organisation rather than as an elitist clique.

Facilities

The appropriate venue for a Think Tank meeting resembles that for a scenario day-dreaming session. It is often most efficient for the participants to assemble for dinner the evening before the meeting proper. The meeting itself should be conducted in a suitable room equipped with all the usual visual aids. If the group is large, syndicate rooms may be necessary for small-group work.

Number of participants

It is difficult to be prescriptive on this issue, since a group's size depends on:
- the nature of its task
- the size of the organisation (e.g. a multi-national organisation would require more Think Tank members than, say, a local business)
- the willingness of the organisation to deploy resources to this type of project.

User's comments

In practice, a group of fewer than six people is rarely large enough to be effective. Similarly, ten to twelve people seems to be an upper limit, unless the Think Tank is divided from the start into a series of subgroups, each with specific objectives.

Roles

Leader. The leader of a Think Tank, like that of a scenario day-dreaming session, should be well-versed both in the various creativity techniques and in organising and facilitating creativity groups. Initially, if such a person cannot be found within the organisation, an

User's comments

outside facilitator may need to be engaged. However, this should only be a temporary measure lasting as long as is necessary to develop the skills and experience of a leader from inside the organisation. Since the tasks associated with leading the Think Tank will be additional to this leader's other responsibilities within the organisation, it may be appropriate to rotate the leadership every six months in order to prevent the role becoming too burdensome for one individual.

Any Think Tank leader should possess:
■ emotional maturity
■ the attitudes characteristic of a creative individual (see pages 62–66)
■ good communication skills, both written and verbal
■ breadth of experience, both within and outside the organisation
■ a record of creative problem-solving
■ a capacity for hard work
■ the ability to think laterally and to foster this ability in others
■ experience of leading small, non-hierarchical groups
■ an understanding of group dynamics and develoment.

The leader's responsibilities include:
■ planning meetings, preparing agendas and ensuring that participants are fully briefed in good time before each meeting
■ maintaining contact with group members between meetings to sustain motivation and enthusiasm
■ leading meetings and allocating specific tasks among participants or sub-groups
■ reporting back to the Think Tank's sponsors and negotiating for additional resources, if necessary
■ summarising proceedings and circulating minutes.

Scribe: Minutes of proceedings are essential to maintain continuity between meetings. It is preferable that the minute-taker is a Think

Tank participant rather than an outsider who might have difficulty understanding the content of the meeting and the 'culture' of the group. The scribe's role may be rotated among participants if it proves to be too demanding for one person to handle on a continuing basis.

Members: Since a Think Tank is a permanent (or at least long-term) body, it is crucial that participants are very carefully selected at the outset, in order to avoid disruptive fluctuations in membership or the awkward necessity of asking an unsuitable participant to retire from the group. Think Tank members should possess enthusiasm, ability and commitment to the goals of the group, and as many of the qualities of highly creative individuals as possible.

In addition they should:

- demonstrate high levels of emotional maturity, personal autonomy and diligence
- be able to work with others
- have a wide variety of outside interests.

Optimists make better members than pessimists. Individuals who have changed direction in their careers or their roles within the organisation can often contribute a valuable breadth of experience to the group. Finally a balance between literate and numerate members can provide a salutary stimulus to the creative functioning of a Think Tank.

In selecting the members of a Think Tank, it is wise to supplement subjective appraisals of potential members' personal attributes and records with a more systematic evaluation. Figure 25 shows a simple screening matrix where one axis represents a candidate's attractiveness as a group member and the other his or her compatibility with the group's needs.

Examples of criteria for compatibility with Think Tank aims
- Personal commitment to Think Tank success
- Optimism
- Willingness to give time to the group
- Specific knowledge about problems under review
- Good relationships with other group members

Examples of criteria for member's attractiveness
- Past experience/skills
- Age/maturity
- Creative characteristics
- Enthusiasm
- Outside interests

Member's attractiveness

Member's compatibility with Think Tank's aims	High	Medium	Low
	Ideal Members	Next Best	Unsuitable
	Next Best	Keep In Reserve	Unsuitable
	Unsuitable	Unsuitable	Unsuitable

Figure 25 A selection matrix for members of a Think Tank

Procedure

A Think Tank may decide to use or adapt any of the creativity techniques previously described, according to the nature of its tasks and the stage of its proceedings. In addition to the procedures necessary for any particular creativity technique, there are also certain specific arrangements required for the successful management of such a permanent creativity group.

The frequency of meetings depends on the structure of a Think Tank and the nature of its objectives. Meetings should be held sufficiently often to:

User's comments

- develop the group's identity and cohesiveness
- provide a sense of continuity and progress from one session to the next
- maintain a sense of urgency in meeting deadlines.

In practice, monthly meetings generally satisfy these requirements without interfering too much with participants' day-to-day responsibilities. Meetings should be scheduled sufficiently far in advance to allow each participant to arrange to attend. Without full attendance at each session, the successful functioning of a Think Tank will be seriously impaired.

Meetings lasting less than a full day are generally not long enough to allow the group to review and assess its progress so far and to make further headway. It is advisable for members to assemble for dinner the evening before the scheduled meeting, in order to renew social contacts, re-establish identity as a creative group, and begin the morning session refreshed and already focused on the business at hand.

An agenda is essential to provide structure and establish clear short-term objectives against which the progress of each session can be evaluated. It is crucial that Think Tank meetings are not allowed to degenerate into aimless gatherings at which the same old problems and issues are reiterated without any progress being made. Agendas for meetings should be prepared and distributed well in advance, together with any necessary papers and the minutes of the last meeting.

A Think Tank should review its own progress at intervals of approximately six months. It should critically evaluate its general performance, achievement of objectives, and overall creativity, and explore ways in which individual and group contributions can be improved. If tackled rigorously and systematically, such periodic appraisals can help maintain morale, motivation and concentration on the group's goals.

User's comments

A typical agenda for a Think Tank meeting could look as follows:

The illustration is based on the assumption that the Think Tank's main task is to develop a vision for the firm's long-term strategic direction

	Theme	Detailed activities
Day I 17.30–19.00	**Assembly of members** **Summary of previous meeting** —Progress made and lessons learnt **Objectives of current meeting** —Discuss, review and agree upon next day's agenda and approach	Leader to provide a brief summary of previous meeting in order to help members 're-enter' into the spirit of the unit's work. Objectives for the next day's proceedings must be clearly stated
19.00–21.00	**Working dinner**	Main aims of the dinner are —To help the members to shed anxieties and preoccupation relating to their respective routine work —To stimulate a re-entry to a 'Creative Mode'
Day II 09.00–10.30	**The future environment for our type of business** The impact of changes in: —Demographics —Anticipated life style.	Previous meeting explored scenarios based on changes likely to take place in 'life style', technology and demography. Today Mr S J, economist/ statistician, will take the chair and report on the outcome of his own analysis based on the literature he scanned
10.30–11.00	**Break**	
11.00–12.45	**The future environment** (continued) Group summary of potential threats and opportunities 5–10 years hence	Group to explore, debate and agree on trends based on scenario-daydreaming method
12.45–14.00	**Working lunch**	Continue discussion regarding group's final view of future environment

14.00–15.30	**Our response to these challenges**
	
	Screen and evaluate proactive strategies
		Group to consider alternative strategies aimed at meeting the challenges and opportunities presented by the future environment as stated by the team
		
		Use: Brainstorming
		        Morphological analysis
		        Scenario-daydreaming
		
		Allocate time to screening ideas

15.30–16.00	**Break**	
16.00–17.30	**Strategy search** (continued) Identify most suitable strategies for further exploration and development	Screen and evaluate every idea against pre-determined criteria of 'attractiveness' and against criteria of 'compatibility'

When a large number of ideas has been generated, the process of converting creative thinking into successful innovation can begin. This is the stage at which practical evaluation techniques should be applied, for without adequate screening procedures an organisation will fail to reap the benefits from its efforts to promote creativity. Critical analysis, which may usefully be suspended during the idea-generating phase, must be reintroduced in order to sift the few superior ideas from the many. Screening represents an essential step in the process of transforming a large quantity of possibilities into a small number of winning innovations.

An organisation's screening procedures must be carefully developed in advance as part of an integrated programme for encouraging innovation, which, as we have seen, should also include the development of an appropriate organisational climate and communication system. The programme's sponsors must decide:

- who screens the ideas
- the stages or intervals at which ideas are evaluated
- the criteria of assessment
- which screening techniques to use.

According to the size and circumstances of the organisation, screening may be undertaken by:

- creative groups themselves, who assess their own ideas in the final stages of idea-generating sessions
- evaluation panels (as in the case of ideas generated by suggestion schemes)
- other groups, such as teams of departmental managers.

It may be appropriate for the evaluation team to assess ideas at regular intervals, for example on a monthly, quarterly or six-monthly basis. This type of periodic assessment is particularly suitable in the management of suggestion schemes, where regular evaluation and feedback are required to maintain interest and motivation in the target audience. Alternatively, screening may occur intermittently, when the reservoir of ideas is considered sufficiently full to make evaluation a practicable exercise. In such cases it is useful to bear in mind that generally only one successful innovation emerges from every fifty or sixty possibilities assessed.

Setting the criteria for assessment

Possible innovations must be evaluated not only for their inherent attractiveness and originality, but also for their feasibility within the organisational context, that is, for the ease and practicality of implementing them and for their compatibility with the organisation's aims and resources. Every screening technique discussed in this section involves judging ideas against a set of predetermined company-specific concerns and circumstances. These criteria will vary from one organisation to the next, but normally relate to such general considerations as:

- the organisation's mission and objectives
- corporate image
- financial resources
- human resources
- the specific need or problem which the innovation is intended to solve.

Setting these company-related criteria in advance is part of the essential developmental work which an organisation must undertake in order to launch and sustain an effective programme of creativity and innovation. The more carefully such criteria are defined, the more fruitful the organisation's efforts to identify successful innovations are likely to be. The needs and concerns of every department or function within the organisation must be taken into consideration in determining appropriate assessment criteria. If an innovation is analysed against the widest possible range of company-wide considerations (rather than, for example, merely those of the marketing or finance department), it stands a greater chance both of being successful in itself and of winning support throughout the organisation.

The screening techniques described in this section represent a range of assessment mechanisms which may be used as part of systematic and practical evaluation procedures. They include:

- the Spider Diagram
- the screening matrix
- the screening algorithm
- weighted comparative evaluation
- force-field analysis
- negative brainstorming
- the How-How Diagram.

The Spider Diagram

Participants in creative idea-generating sessions often notice that although ideas initially emerge in random order during such exercises, with hindsight they often seem to cluster into a limited number of general categories. Indeed, the fact that this happens is a good indication that a group's creative potential has been successfully stimulated and participants' imaginations are sparking off one another. Even the results of quite open-ended activities such as suggestion schemes or exploratory creative work tend to fall into a limited number of definable areas, usually no more than a maximum of fifteen.

This tendency for ideas to group themselves into logical strands may be compared to a spider's web which, although woven in a circular and seemingly haphazard fashion, nevertheless is organised into a number of identifiable segments. While it is unnecessary to develop this comparison beyond a loose analogy, the image of the spider web suggests a useful method for organising a number of apparently disparate ideas into more manageable segments or categories. It is far easier to evaluate large numbers of ideas in groups rather than individually. A Spider Diagram such as the one shown on page 142 represents a useful preliminary sorting tool because it provides a visual way of grouping ideas into related clusters.

Procedure

Step *Sorting the ideas.* After a suitable number of ideas has been assembled, they are grouped into the general and usually relatively obvious categories which they suggest. For example, in a warm-up brainstorming exercise asking participants to list as many uses as possible for broken teacups, a group might generate the following ideas (among others):

- use fragments as materials for mosaics
- use to line the bottoms of flower pots to aid soil drainage
- scatter the sharpest pieces in front of doors or windows as crude burglar deterrants
- use sharp shards as slug barriers for tender plants
- grind up and use as a component of sandpaper
- use the handles as coat hooks
- use the shards as testing devices for puncture-proof tyres
- turn upside down and use as decorative edging for paths and flower beds.

These suggestions might be grouped into the following categories:

- gardening uses
- barriers
- decorative uses
- domestic uses
- industrial applications.

Step *Filling in the diagram.* Each category is allocated a segment of the Spider Diagram and individual ideas are listed in the appropriate segment (or segments). The spider web should be imagined as being sufficiently elastic to accommodate whatever number of ideas logically belongs in any particular segment. It is acceptable to produce a lopsided web which, for example, contains 20 entries in one segment and only 3 in another. Figure 27 shows how the ideas from the previous example would be listed in a Spider Diagram. Notice that several of the ideas logically belong in more than one category and thus appear in each relevant segment of the diagram. This ensures that such ideas are given fair consideration in each of the various contexts to which they relate.

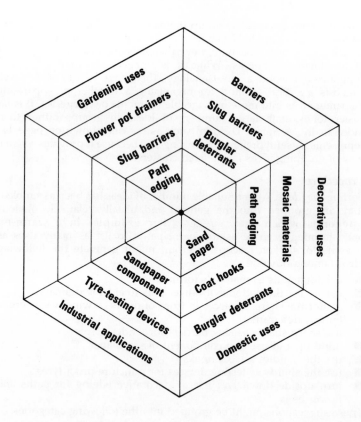

Figure 27 An example of a Spider Diagram

 Step 3 *Evaluating the categories.* Each category or segment of the diagram may be assessed according to the various relevant criteria determined by the organisation's screening committee. Certain entire categories might thus be eliminated as impracticable without the need to consider each individual idea in the segment, although this will not necessarily occur in every case.

Step 4 *Evaluating the ideas.* The ideas in each suitable segment may then be screened using one or more of the assessment techniques discussed later in this section. After the best ideas in each segment have been identified, they may be evaluated against one another so that the best overall ideas emerge.

Spider Diagram Worksheet

Assign a category to each segment of the diagram and list ideas in the segment to which they relate. Ideas may be listed in more than one segment if this is appropriate. The diagram may be expanded as necessary to accommodate all the ideas to be included.

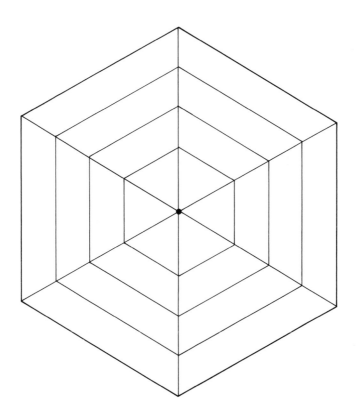

Screening Matrix

The screening matrix is a simple but effective method which allows ideas to be judged simultaneously in terms of both their inherent attractiveness and their practicality. These two considerations form the axes of a two-dimensional matrix such as the one shown in Figure 28. The horizontal axis represents the level of creative excellence when an idea is considered solely on its own merits. The vertical axis represents an idea's degree of compatibility with the aims and resources of the organisation. Together, both sets of criteria indicate how suitable any idea would be for development into a winning innovation.

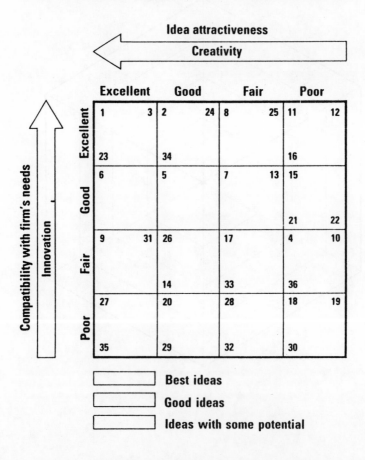

Figure 28 An example of a screening matrix

Procedure

Step

Defining criteria. The criteria for both the 'Creativity' and 'Innovation' axes are defined according to the nature of the need or problem to be addressed. For example, the inherent creativity of ideas might be assessed on the basis of:

- market appeal
- originality
- simplicity
- ease of production or implementation
- ease of protecting (e.g. patenting) the idea
- outstanding design features
- cost-effectiveness.

The ideas' potential to become successful innovations within the context of the sponsoring organisation might be judged according to their compatibility with:

- corporate objectives such as long-term marketing, financial or staffing strategies
- corporate image
- available funding
- available skills and personnel
- available technical expertise
- existing distribution channels
- the problem's priority within the organisation.

Step

Evaluating the ideas. Each idea under consideration is assigned a code number (to save writing it out in full in the matrix) and evaluated separately as 'excellent', 'good', 'fair' or 'poor' in meeting the criteria for both the 'Creativity' and 'Innovation' axes. If assesment is undertaken by a group, participants should assign a numerical rating to each idea: from 4 for 'excellent' to 1 for 'poor'. This allows the ratings to be averaged and the calibre of each idea to be accurately identified as excellent to poor on each scale. The screening team might wish to discuss the ratings of each idea, especially in cases where discrepancies exist. This is not so much to achieve consensus as to allow evaluators to clarify their thoughts as to the merits of particular ideas.

Step

Listing ideas on the matrix. The code number of each idea is then written in the relevant cell of the matrix, according to the idea's ratings against both the 'Creativity' and 'Innovation' criteria. In this way the few outstanding ideas which rate highly in both dimensions may be identified immediately. The ideas which appear in the top left 'excellent/excellent' cell are most worthy of implementation, while the 'excellent/good' and 'good/excellent' ideas, although second-best, deserve further consideration.

Screening matrix worksheet

After assessing each idea under consideration according to the relevant criteria on both the 'Creativity' and 'Innovation' axes, write the code number of each idea in the appropriate cell of the matrix.

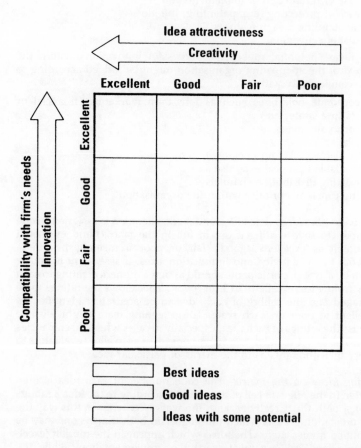

Quantified screening matrix

The results of a screening matrix are often more meaningful if the somewhat imprecise and subjective ratings from 'excellent' to 'poor' are replaced by numerical values. The screening procedure remains the same except that each axis is divided into 10 segments so the matrix contains 100 cells or rating points, as shown in Figure 29. Each idea is given a score from 1 to 10 on each axis, the two scores are multiplied, and the idea's code number is listed in the appropriate cell of the matrix.

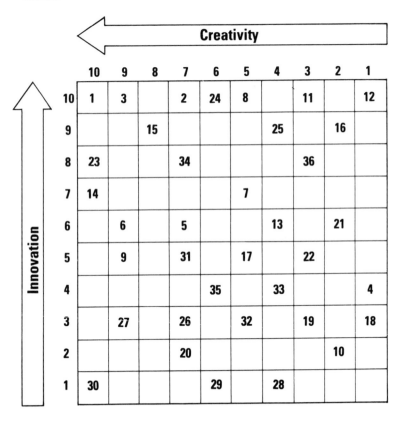

Figure 29 A quantified screening matrix

This system allows the expression of finer degrees of differentiation in the assessment of ideas and permits the ratings of a team of assessors to be accurately averaged. It is especially useful when a large number of ideas must be screened, because the range of ratings it offers is both wide and precise. In cases of preliminary assessment, for example, ideas with overall scores of less than 60 may be eliminated from further assessment proceedings.

A word of caution, however: it is important to recognise that merely assigning numerical values to assessments does not automatically make these assessments more scientific or foolproof. They are still based on human judgements and can only be as accurate as the judgements themselves. The merit of the quantified screening matrix is that it demonstrates quickly and visually the relative suitability of a number of ideas once those ideas have been discussed and evaluated by the screening panel.

Quantified Screening Matrix Worksheet

After assessing each idea under consideration according to the relevant criteria on both the 'Creativity' and 'Innovation' axes, write the code number of each idea in the appropriate cell of the matrix.

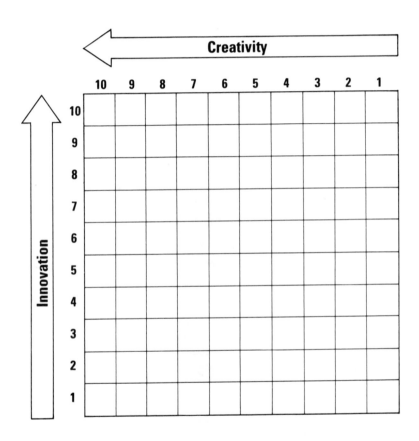

Screening algorithm

Another visual and systematic assessment method is the screening algorithm or flow chart, which sifts ideas according to predetermined relevant criteria. Figure 30 shows an example of a screening algorithm.

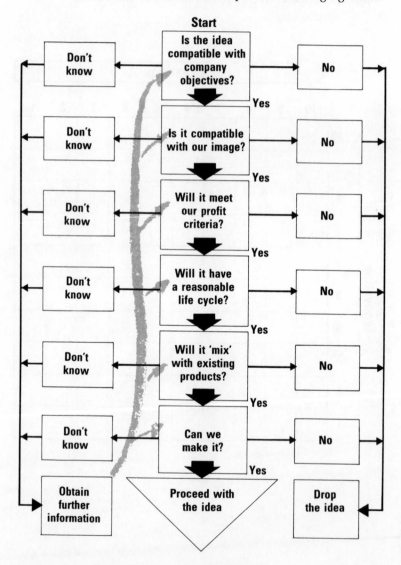

Figure 30 An example of a screening algorithm

Once a suitable algorithm has been devised, it is a relatively simple matter to take each idea as far as it will go along the flow path. As with many screening techniques, the most demanding task in using this method is the preparatory work of determining the appropriate criteria from which to construct the algorithm.

Screening Algorithm Worksheet

Fill in the blank boxes with relevant assessment questions and use the algorithm to evaluate each idea under consideration. The algorithm may be extended as much as necessary to include all the questions appropriate to any particular screening flow path.

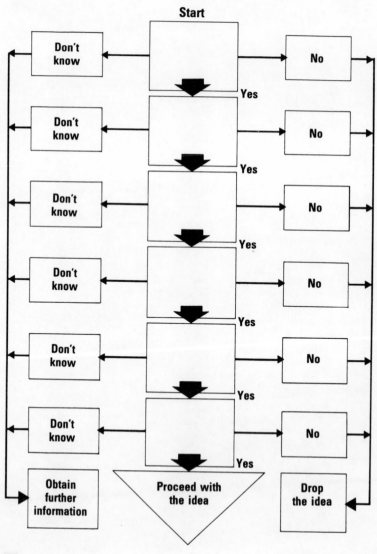

Weighted comparative evaluation

The screening techniques examined so far have assumed that each individual assessment criterion bears equal importance in determining the merits of an idea. However, this is seldom true, and more accurate evaluations may be obtained when these various criteria are ascribed relative 'weights' or degrees of importance. The Comparative Evaluation Table shown in Figure 31 illustrates a practical system for judging ideas against weighted criteria.

	Criteria	Weight	Idea 1 Rating	Idea 1 Score	Idea 2 Rating	Idea 2 Score	Idea 3 Rating	Idea 3 Score	Idea 4 Rating	Idea 4 Score	Idea 5 Rating	Idea 5 Score
Idea attractiveness	Market appeal	.15	6	0.9	5	0.75	8	1.2	3	0.45	7	1.05
	Originality	.10	2	0.2	4	0.4	5	0.5	10	1.0	6	0.6
	Ease of production	.10	5	0.5	7	0.7	4	0.4	3	0.3	8	0.8
	Cost-effectiveness	.15	8	1.2	3	0.45	7	1.05	5	0.75	7	1.05
Compatibility with organisation	Financial resources	.20	3	0.6	5	1.0	7	1.4	9	1.8	6	1.2
	Human resources	.10	5	0.5	6	0.6	2	0.2	4	0.4	8	0.8
	Corporate image	.05	6	0.3	2	0.1	3	0.15	4	0.2	5	0.25
	Solves high-priority need	.15	4	0.6	8	1.2	5	0.75	7	1.05	9	1.35
	Total:			4.8		5.2		5.65		5.95		7.1

Procedure

Step 1 *Listing and weighting criteria.* The screening team determines the criteria against which each idea is to be assessed and assigns a relative weight to each criterion so that the sum total of all the weights equals 1.

Step 2 *Rating the ideas.* The screening team evaluates each idea by rating it between 0 and 10 against each criterion (with 10 indicating that the idea fulfils the criterion excellently and 0 indicating that it does not fulfil it at all). These ratings are then multiplied by each criterion's weight to give a score. The scores for each idea are added together to give an overall assessment figure. The idea with the highest total score has been judged to be the best idea.

Weighted Evaluation Table Worksheet

Identify the relevant criteria under both 'Idea attractiveness' and 'Compatibility with organisation', then determine the weight of each criterion. The number of criteria in each (or either) category may be increased if appropriate. Rank each idea against each weighted criterion and add up the total score at the bottom of the column. The idea with the highest total score is the best idea.

		Idea 1		Idea 2		Idea 3		Idea 4		Idea 5	
	Weight	Rating	Score	Rating	Score	Rating	Score	Rating	Score	Rating	Score
Criteria											
Idea attractiveness — **Market appeal**											
Originality											
Ease of production											
Cost-effectiveness											
Compatibility with organisation — **Financial resources**											
Human resources											
Corporate image											
Solves high-priority need											
Total:											

Force-field analysis

Force-field analysis was introduced in Section 3 (pages 46-48) as a tool for assessing an organisation's receptivity to creativity and innovation. The same technique can be adapted for idea-screening. In this application the force-field diagram is used as a means of predicting the probable impact and success of a potential innovation. Driving and restraining forces are anticipated and their relative importance assessed in order to forecast the likely consequences of implementing an idea.

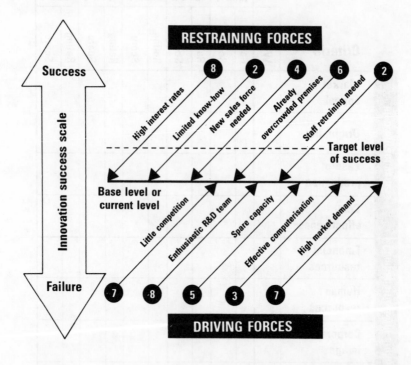

Figure 32 An example of force-field analysis as an idea-screening technique

As with other screening techniques, force-field analysis is most useful if the 'force-field' of company-specific influencing factors is comprehensively identified and discussed. Since the pros and cons of each idea are examined individually in some depth, this technique is usually most appropriate in the later stages of idea-screening, when the 5 or 6 most promising candidates for implementation have already been identified.

Step *Identifying the Driving and Restraining Forces.* Considering each idea individually, the screening panel lists and discusses the factors which would promote its success and those which would inhibit it. These factors are inserted into the diagram as either driving forces which would raise the potential innovation's chances of success, or restraining forces which would lower them. The driving forces are represented by arrows pushing up the projected level of success, while the restraining forces are designated by arrows pushing it down.

Step *Weighting the Driving and Restraining Forces.* The evaluation team analyses each of the influencing factors, attempting to reach agreement about its importance in relation to the other factors. When the relative strengths of the various forces have been determined, a numerical value from 1 to 10 is assigned to each factor (with 1 representing the least significant, and 10 the most significant). These 'weights' are written in the circle at the base of each arrow. (It is unnecessary to assign a different weight to each factor – what matters is the relationships among them. If, for example, several factors have equal weight, this significant fact should be accurately reflected in the force-field diagram.)

Step *Assessing the force-field diagram.* The screening team compares the force-field diagrams of each idea under consideration and selects the idea or ideas most likely to become successful innovations. A carefully completed force-field diagram should show at a glance the likely future success of any proposed innovation. If the anticipated restraining forces are considerably greater than the driving forces, for example, the idea is almost certainly a non-starter and should be rejected before valuable resources are wasted on it. If, on the other hand, the supporting and inhibiting factors are more evenly balanced, or are more heavily weighted towards the positive factors, the idea is a more serious contender for implementation.

As the final stage of the assessment process, the screening committee should consider ways in which:
■ the most promising ideas could be improved still further
■ the driving forces could be strengthened
■ the restraining forces could be lessened or removed.

Like scenario day-dreaming (discussed in Section 5, pages 113-23), force-field analysis is a predictive technique which can signal possible future problems. Since this technique helps evaluators assess the range of factors which would impinge on any particular innovation, it is useful in screening out weak ideas and identifying strong ones. Moreover, it provides evaluators with a sufficiently realistic forecast of implementation to allow them to modify a promising idea in light of relevant forces and/or (when circumstances permit) to seek to ameliorate the hostile elements of the context into which it is to be introduced. If both potential innovations and the 'force fields' surrounding them are regarded as dynamic and alterable rather then static, force-field analysis becomes a technique not merely for screening ideas, but also for improving and facilitating the implementation of the most promising ones.

Force-field Analysis Worksheet

Identify the driving and restraining forces for the idea under consideration and list these along the appropriate arrows. More arrows may be added if necessary. Assign a weight from 1 to 10 to each factor (where 1 indicates least importance and 10 indicates greatest importance). What does the diagram reveal about the idea's chances of success? Are there ways in which the driving forces could be strengthened or the restraining forces diminished or removed?

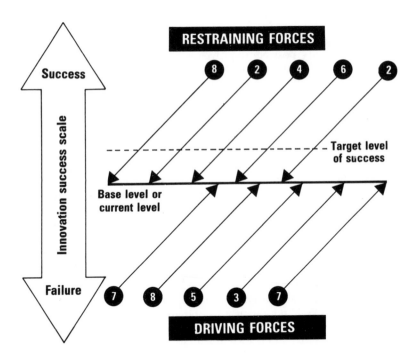

Negative brainstorming

Like force-field analysis, negative brainstorming is a method for predicting the possible drawbacks of a proposed innovation, and is most appropriate for the later stages of idea-screening when a few, pre-screened ideas can be given extensive consideration. As the name suggests, this method uses the brainstorming technique described in Section 5, but instead of asking 'In how many ways can this problem be solved?', this approach asks, 'In how many ways can this idea fail?' The screening panel uses the brainstorming technique to play devil's advocate, forecasting as many potential problems in the implementation of an innovation as possible.

As well as identifying genuine drawbacks which might cause a proposed innovation to be rejected, deliberately exploring the awkward question of why an idea won't work allows an evaluation team to identify possible improvements. It also permits a screening panel to anticipate objections from possible investors, senior management or the organisation at large, so that genuinely worthwhile ideas can be presented in such a way that these objections are answered before they are raised.

How-How Diagram

Another technique useful in the later stages of idea-screening is the How-How Diagram. This works in a similar way to the Why-Why Diagram discussed on pages 85–6, except that instead of analysing the reasons underlying a particular problem, it focuses on the ways in which a proposed solution may be implemented. Because this technique is detailed and time-consuming, it is only practical to apply it to the most promising ideas which have already successfully passed through several earlier stages of screening. The evaluation panel attempts to identify the steps necessary to transform the idea from a proposal on paper to a fully-operational innovation. Each step is thoroughly discussed and broken down into further steps by asking the question 'How?', until the most workable procedure is agreed and further analysis is no longer a meaningful or productive exercise. A simplified example of a How-How Diagram is shown in Figure 33. Note that this diagram is incomplete, as the question 'How?' can still identify essential steps in the implementation of the proposed solution.

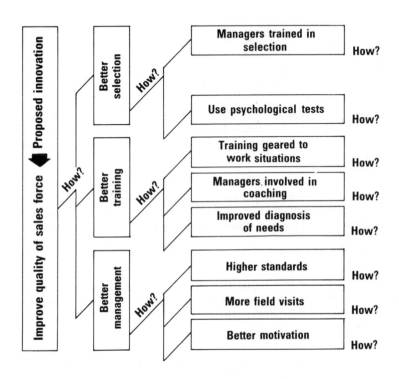

Figure 33 An example of a How-How diagram

Taking a suggested innovation through the detailed stages of its implementation forces an evaluation panel to confront the practical issues involved and often highlights possible problems and discrepancies between organisational aims and resources on the one hand, and the innovation's requirements on the other. As with negative brainstorming, this may have several results:

- rejection of the idea as impracticable
- suggestions for improving the idea so that it matches existing resources more closely
- strategies for modifying or increasing organisational resources so that implementation may occur.

If used in this last way, the How-How Diagram operates not merely as a screening technique but also as a bridge between idea-screening and the formulation of a detailed strategy for the implementtion of an innovation. Methods for monitoring the success of innovations are discussed in Section 7.

Procedure

Step *Listing the initial steps to implemetation.* The screening panel discusses the proposed innovation in order to identify the initial steps needed to implement it within the organisation. The innovation and recommended steps are written in the appropriate blanks in the How-How Diagram.

Step *Breaking down the steps.* The screening team considers each step individually, breaking it down into its detailed, constituent stages by repeatedly asking 'How?' it might be achieved. Each stage is recorded in the diagram.

Step *Analysing the diagram.* When each step has been drawn out to its logical limit, the screening panel examines the completed diagram for recurring elements, which should be circled or marked with asterisks. These tend to indicate the most crucial stages in the process of implementation. After further discussion and analysis, the panel may decide to draw up a critical path diagram for the implementation process, showing the relationships and proper sequence in which the steps should be undertaken.

How-How Diagram Worksheet

Working backwards from the proposed innovation, list the initial steps necessary for its implementation, then the successive steps necessary to achieve the initial steps, until a logical starting point for implementation has been identified. Is each step compatible with available resources? If not, should the idea be rejected or improved, or can sufficient additional resources be made available?

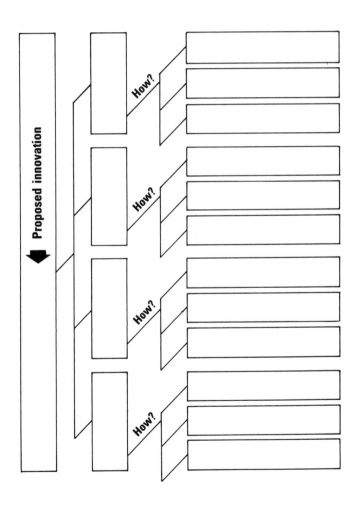

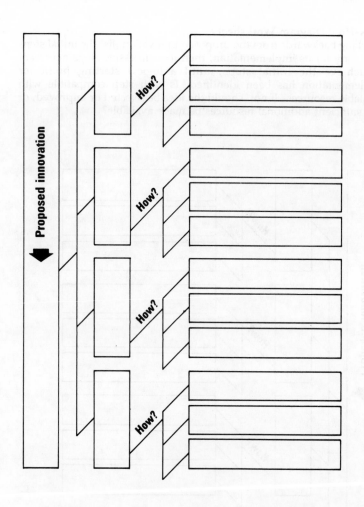

Managing the process

It should be evident by now that 'Innovation' does not happen by itself. It has to be managed, nurtured and controlled in a systematic way. Ideally the impetus and stimulation must come from top management. Companies in which senior management is totally committed to the process of creativity and innovation stand a far better chance of generating successful innovations.

At this point it would be useful to review the various components that help a company to manage the innovation process more effectively.

Figure 26 provides a diagrammatic model of the elements which must be developed in the pursuit of innovation.

Figure 26   The management of innovation: an integrated approach

A brief description of each of the eight elements shown should help the reader to audit his or her firm's ability to attain and/or improve excellence in this area.

Climate

The climate for innovation is right when every person in the firm – senior or junior – 'thinks', 'talks' and 'acts' creatively.

Removal of barriers

Each organisation suffers from a number of barriers to innovation, such as bureaucracy, obsession with the 'bottom line', a 'not invented here' syndrome and so on. All these must be identified and removed.

Creative planning process

If innovation must start at the top, the bosses must demonstrate their ability to develop an innovative vision and plan the future direction of the firm in a creative way.

Developing sources of ideas

We saw in earlier sections that there are many sources of ideas. An innovative firm ensures that such sources are fully tapped.

Communication procedures

A system must be established to ensure that every member of the organisation knows how and to whom to convey ideas.

Motivational stimuli

Motivational stimuli can act as a powerful booster to innovation. Such stimuli need not be of monetary or material nature. A pat on the shoulder or a badge of approval can achieve the same aim.

Idea evaluation procedures

These must be installed and, ideally, communicated to the firm's personnel. Knowledge of the criteria of attractiveness (as described in Section 6) can help to improve the conversion rate between ideas and innovations.

Managing innovation

The best stimulus to creativity is the knowledge that ideas are being implemented from time to time. Monitoring such successes and identifying the lessons learned represent the logical culmination of the whole cycle.

Managing innovation worksheet

Mark the number that best fits your assessment of each element, with 1 representing the lowest and 5 the highest evaluation.

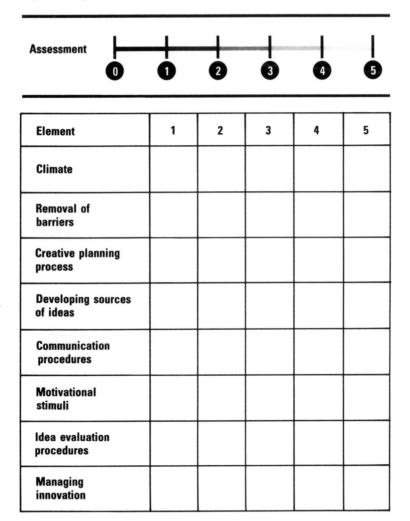

Element	1	2	3	4	5
Climate					
Removal of barriers					
Creative planning process					
Developing sources of ideas					
Communication procedures					
Motivational stimuli					
Idea evaluation procedures					
Managing innovation					

The aim of the worksheet is to identify areas within an organisation in which intensive corrective measures need to be undertaken. Any element which scores 3 or lower is particularly suitable for such special efforts.

Monitoring results

An important part of the process of managing innovation is the systematic listing of the successful implementation of ideas during a given period. Most organisations monitor their actual results such as sales, profits, market share and so on, against pre-defined plans or budgets. A similar procedure must be applied to the management of innovation. The following two worksheets are designed to help an organisation monitor and analyse the number and success of all innovations implemented during the period of a year.

Monitoring innovations

The following innovation monitoring worksheet allows an organisation to list all the innovations attained during the year, and contains details of:
- the date of implementation
- the nature of each innovation
- the team or group of people responsible for the implementation of each innovation.

Such information is valuable in helping to identify ways to improve future efforts to promote innovation.

Innovation monitoring worksheet

Innovation number	Date implemented	Description of innovation	Team/people responsible for implementation

Analysing innovations

The following innovation analysis worksheet is simply a more detailed version of the monitoring innovation worksheet and contains
- a description of each innovation
- the date of implementation
- the benefits gained over a specified period
- further work still needed to exploit the innovation fully
- lessons learned

The last element is very valuable. Organisations that seek to manage the innovation process effectively can learn from each achievement (or failure) better ways of:
- managing creative groups
- screening ideas efficiently
- shortening the period between the generation of ideas and the implementation of innovations
- improving the conversion rate between ideas and innovations.

Figure 27 shows an example of a partially completed innovation analysis worksheet.

Innovation Analysis Worksheet

Innovation number	Description of innovation	Date implemented	Benefits attained (over period to be specified)	Further work needed	Lessons learned

Figure 27   A sample innovation analysis worksheet

Innovation analysis worksheet

Innovation number	Description of innovation	Date implemented	Benefits attained (over a period to be specified)	Further work needed	Lessons learned
1					
2					
3	Toothbrush with a thin reinforcing steel rod inside the plastic handle	25/6/89	1. While cost of production rose by about 8% our new product can command 20% higher prices. 2. No complaints about quality received (as against 3% complaints about broken handles with standard brushes). 3. Profits of the department improved by 25%	1. Awareness of the new product is to be increased from its present level of 5% to 10% 2. Patent application to be pursued more vigorously.	The idea emerged during a metaphorical analysis session. One of the participants drew an analogy between our problem and the use of steel rods in reinforced concrete beams. We learned that: 1. metaphorical analysis it is a valuable technique. 2. Problem-solving teams can easily relate to such a technique.

Monitoring the conversion rate between ideas and innovations

One final procedure which can help management to monitor the conversion rate between ideas and innovations is the innovation conversion rate worksheet. Figure 28 shows an example of a partially completed worksheet.

Innovation Conversion Rate Worksheet

Year	Ideas screened	Average per employee	Number of ideas implemented	Percentage implemented	Remarks
1987	1,200	0.5	12	1%	
1988	4,800	2	100	4.8%	
1989	12,000	5	1,200	10%	

Figure 28   A sample innovation conversion rate worksheet

Innovation Conversion Rate Worksheet

Year	Ideas screened	Average per employee	Number of ideas implemented	Percentage implemented	Remarks

It must be recalled that on average it is necessary to consider 50–60 ideas to find one viable innovaiton. The aim of the following worksheet is to monitor the organisation's actual performance in this regard. Through practice, training and persistent coaching, it is possible for an organisation to improve its ideas-to-innovation ratio. This may be achieved if the criteria for assessment are widely known, so that a considerable amount of initial screening and evaluation is undertaken by the people who actually generate the ideas. Instead of submitting half-baked ideas, people tend to reflect upon and pre-screen their suggestions before putting them forward for an evaluation panel to consider. This results in a more efficient conversion rate and means that to some extent the centre of gravity of the process shifts from the evaluation team back to the idea generators. Such a situation can only be achieved, however, if all the eight elements of an innovative organisation (as described in Figure 26) are in place and operating successfully.

INDEX